WHERE JESUS WALKS

WHERE JESUS WALKS

By

Ruth Youngdahl Nelson

AUGSBURG PUBLISHING HOUSE
Minneapolis   Minnesota

WHERE JESUS WALKS

Scripture quotations are from the Revised Standard Version of the Bible, copyright 1946 and 1952 by the Division of Christian Education of the National Council of Churches.

Hymns from the *Service Book and Hymnal* are used by permission of the Commission on the Liturgy and the Hymnal.

The author would like to express her gratitude to Margaret Bukala, who so graciously used vacation time to type this manuscript.

*This book is lovingly dedicated
to the Saturday Evening Bible Class
of the Dhahran Protestant Fellowship*

Table of Contents

Introduction

It was at our international Bible class that I awakened with a jolt. Oh, there had been tremors in my consciousness at other times when I found myself singing a hymn blithely, and then suddenly becoming aware of the real import of the words. But on this Saturday evening, out on the Arabian desert, the thing that happened hit my comfortable soul like an earthquake. All through the following week I was dogged by the thought: Do I really mean it? Would I?

It was as simple as this. In our joyous singing time we proposed that these friends in their lovely saris learn a Swahili song that had been taught us by some friends from Tanzania. So, strumming a ukulele, we proceeded to sing:

> *Jesu, Jesu, nimfuate Jesus,*
> *Popote, popote, atembeapo.*
> *Jesu, Jesu, nimfuate Jesus,*
> *Popote, popote, atakaponituma.*

I noticed that the faces were wreathed in smiles. Then one of the class members said, "We know that in Hindi," and spontaneously they picked up the chorus that had just been sung in Swahili. One of our friends added, "Why don't we sing it in English?" At this I raised my eyebrows, because, although I knew the meaning of the words, I had never heard them sung in English. I soon found myself picking my way through the English words with the rest of them:

> Follow, follow, I will follow Jesus,
> Anywhere, anywhere, anywhere he leads.
> Follow, follow, I will follow Jesus,
> Anywhere, anywhere, anywhere that he may go.

So in Saudi Arabia I learned to sing the Swahili song in English from my Indian friends.

Something else happened to me than just this language experience. How the Holy Spirit can use a simple chorus! How he can use a Bach chorale! Maybe we ought to say how he can use any medium that is given to him! I was deeply bothered all week by the fact that hundreds of times I had sung that song in Swahili, had taught the words to a number of groups, and yet had basically evaded the full import of their meaning. "I will follow Jesus anywhere." As I thought through what this might mean, another question popped in: "Where would Jesus go?" This was the beginning of the book *Where Jesus Walks*.

Notice that the verb is in the present. Not only long ago on those Palestinian paths did Jesus walk into people's lives. The Eternal Now that he is, is as surely entering into hearts with his transforming presence today if the way is not barred. Here is the big "If."

You see this journey is costly! It means giving all of yourself, believing that his will is best for your life. It means honesty: with yourself first, then with God, and then with your fellowmen. It means disciplining yourself, often against your natural desires, to take time to be exposed to his presence, to follow the rugged path he walks.

There are no words to describe the joy of the journey to those who are willing to pay the price.

Are you ready to go?

CHAPTER ONE

To the Land of Prayer

Suppose I were to hand you a passport and a ticket and tell you: "These will take you into a land where burdens are lifted, where the sun breaks through the clouds, where equipment for whatever rough roads may lie ahead is provided," what would your answer be?

To this enticing invitation I would add the witness of contemporaries who are traveling in this land. Listen to this sampling.

A judge, at the time when he was called upon to make a momentous decision, when diverse forces were crowding him and threatening him, withdrew into his inner office to be alone with God. He later witnessed that this was the only thing that kept him sane during those strenuous days.

An executive who was to be a part of a negotiating team between management and labor, used his lunch hour to journey into the Land of Prayer, and was empowered to come into the meeting with such a spirit as to change the whole atmosphere.

A stenographer who was being pressured by an irritated boss, withdrew to the rest room to pray. She came back calm in the knowledge that the Lord would give her patience and skill to do the job at hand.

A harassed mother, who felt that if one more thing were to happen in her household, she would "blow up," was persuaded to join a neighbor in a quiet time of prayer, and returned to her home so changed that her children wondered what had happened to her.

Perhaps at this point we should say a word about some things prayer isn't.

It is not a magic formula that will put a Cadillac at your door when the Lord knows that a Volkswagen would enable you to be a better steward and eliminate strain from your budget.

It is not an easy way of escape from living where God has placed you (or where you in your willfulness have chosen to be).

It is not a soporific to dull your senses to the needs and calamities about you.

On the contrary, it is a discernment that brings values into their right perspective. It is the power that helps us to face life's difficulties with courage and hope. It is the means by which we can see the world as it is and be guided into the how of being a part of the solution rather than the problem.

The Holy Spirit of God is primed through prayer. We bring to God's well, as we turn to him in prayer, a cup of our faith. Then the miracle happens. His living water flows freely into our souls to quench the thirst that nothing else can satisfy. John was baptizing, and while Jesus was praying, the Holy Spirit descended on him in the bodily form of a dove (Luke 3:21).

Someone has said that no chemical analysis of water can take the place of drinking it. How ironic it would be to go to a Bedouin shepherd whose entire body was parched and say: "My good man, let me tell you about water. It is 11.188% by weight hydrogen, and 88.812% oxygen. According to Webster's dictionary, it is the liquid which descends from clouds in rain." Can you see the agony of the man who would have to listen to all this, while his very body was burning from thirst? Maybe you are that Bedouin. Won't you, then, now, pause before the journey continues, and drink? Maybe your gasp will simply be, "God!" Maybe you will want to cry out: "Lord, help me!" Or, "Lord, search me!" If you are to journey deep into this land, such petitions are the point of beginning.

Here it would be helpful to see the pattern of Jesus' life in regard to prayer. Both before and after performing miracles, Jesus retreated alone to a place of prayer. In Mark 1:35 we read: "And in the morning, a great while before dawn, he rose and went out to a lonely place, and there he prayed." What a busy day had preceded this prayer tryst! He had been in the synagogue teaching. While there, a man with an unclean spirit confronted him. Jesus rebuked the unclean spirit, and the man was made whole.

From the synagogue, Jesus and his disciples had gone to Simon's house where the latter's mother-in-law lay ill of a fever. Jesus took her by the hand and healed her so that she was able to minister to them.

But his day was not yet ended, for we are told that in the evening, after sunset, they brought to him all who were ill and possessed of devils. Yet—or should we say, so—he arose early the next morning to pray.

Do you know the joy of stepping into your office, your kitchen, your classroom, with the sense of the Holy Spirit's being with you because you have paused to pray?

Toynbee, the historian, in a section of his masterpiece *A Study of History,* says that each truly great leader has first taken time out and gone off by himself to be alone. During this time they apparently lost their sense of egocentricity and were caught up by a power outside of themselves. God can do almost anything with you, if given a chance.

Jesus used prayer in anticipation of what was to happen. In Luke 6:12 we read that he went to the hills to pray and spent all night in prayer. The next morning he called the disciples to him and named them. Do you journey into the land of prayer before you make decisions? Have you learned how this journey will set your feet on the course you should take? Have you experienced how in this land you are released from the tensions which impair your judgment and make you incapable of objectively seeing goals?

A young friend, mother of three, told what a revelation such an experience had been to her and her husband. He had an opportunity to change firms, and there were many questions involved which they seemed unable to resolve. Almost in desperation the wife said to her husband: "I think we had better pray about this." She told of how their prayers previously had been pretty perfunctory and she was almost embarrassed about making this suggestion. They knelt, the two of them, and cried to God for guidance. On their knees before his all-seeing eyes, values came clear and they were able to make the decision without hesitation. She witnesses to the fact that this opened a whole new avenue of prayer for them.

Look to the Lord again. In Matthew 14:23 we are told that after feeding the five thousand, Jesus retreated to pray. Is verse 14 the key verse, which relates how, after seeing the crowd, the sick, the hungry—the great avalanche of human needs—the Lord needed to go apart to pray?

Today the most common excuse for the lack of a prayer excursion is: "I haven't time." It is significant to note, in the life of Christ, that when the demands were greatest, he withdrew the most in prayer. In Luke 5:15, 16 we read about the great crowds that gathered to hear him to be cured of their ailments. Then we are told that from time to time he would withdraw to lonely places of prayer.

What a false premise the "I haven't time" is! Face it. You find time for the things you really want to do. Could this excuse be a cover up for your not caring, or not believing, or not daring? People miss mountain-top experiences because they don't take time.

On our global travels our outstanding memories have come from times when we extended ourselves to meet some unusual person or to see some particular sight. One such instance comes vividly to mind. We were in a party of Jerusalem pilgrims from Arabia on World Day of Prayer. We thought it would be wonderful to have a Mount of Olives experience on this day. The only time that it could be arranged was for the early morning hour of 5:30. We set our alarms for four-forty-five, and awakened to a cold and somewhat drizzly day. We were thrilled to find some 60 intrepid souls gathered at the top of that sacred mount. What a colorful company! Besides the Indian girls in their saris there were Lebanese, Syrian, and Jordanian friends joining us Americans in becoming a link in this fellowship of prayer.

At first we huddled together in the cold, but as we lifted our voices in "Holy, Holy, Holy" the rain ceased. We experienced an unforgettable hour through Scripture and prayer, so our warmed hearts helped dispel the chill of our bodies. Just as our little service was drawing to a close, the Master Electrician turned the switch, and a glorious shaft of light—orange, and gold, and crimson—broke through the clouds as we were facing east. Spontaneously from overflowing hearts, voices broke into song: "Jesus shall reign where'er the sun, Does its successive journeys run," and then "He's got the whole world in his hands."

When we returned from the mountain to the hotel, we were met by folks to whom the warmth of their beds that morning meant more than this tryst with the One who ascended from that very mount. I suspect that the glow in the eyes of the early risers suggested something of what had been missed.

Are you missing sunrise experiences because your physical comforts are your primary consideration? Have you ever tried to see if the Lord wouldn't more than supply your needs for the day because you journeyed with him into the land of prayer at the day's beginning?

God certainly isn't limited to any time of the day. To pray without ceasing is to be journeying with him all the time. The pattern Jesus set was for special times apart, too, when alone with him our souls can absorb the peace and strength of his presence.

Not long ago a friend shared a hospital experience that had thrilled her. On this particular night she was in a great deal of pain. Previous nights' sedatives had proved unsuccessful in relieving her.

Early evening found her inwardly fretting at the uncomfortable night she was anticipating. Then she began thinking of all the people in her wing. Something of the difficulties of each had been told her. She found herself remembering the occupants in each room in prayer, holding each up to God for a healing blessing. When she had made the rounds in her prayer journey, she fell asleep, without the aid of the pill.

When the nurse stepped in the next morning she said, "Well, how are you this morning?" The ready, warm response was: "Why, I'm fine. I feel the best I have in days. I fell asleep last night like a babe in its mother's arms." "Well, I never," said the nurse. "What's the matter with this wing this morning? In every room I have gone, the answer has been the same. Everybody's feeling just fine." As the nurse left the room, she wondered at the unusual smile on the patient's face.

Travel Guides

1. Set a time and place where you can withdraw and be alone.

2. Search the Scriptures for instructions and guideposts.

3. Share your trip experiences with others.

4. Make the keynote of each day thanksgiving to the great Trail Blazer.

Prayer

Lord, my prayer life has been narrow and confined. So often prayer time has been crowded out. Even when I've taken time, it seems that my prayers have hardly left the ground. I want to be a learner, Lord Jesus. I want to follow you into the land of prayer. Take my hand, and lead the way. Thank you for being a loving and patient Teacher. Amen.

CHAPTER TWO

To the Land of Prayer:

Adoration

In the following chapters we hope to spell out four major avenues whose first letters make an acrostic ACTS. These serve as directive guideposts on our many faceted journey. As Evelyn Underhill has so aptly put it, often our prayers are mere celestial shopping lists. Where does a person begin?

Great vistas would be open to the soul if a person is schooled in the act of adoration. Many times our prayers are weighted down with materialistic requests. An astronomer, looking through his telescope, thought that he had discovered some immense and peculiar inhabitants of the moon. Then he discovered that there were some minute insects on his lens which were responsible for his false assumption. Often we get lost in the maze of our praying because things close at hand obstruct our view into the land of the spirit.

When visiting Prague, we decided that we wanted a first-hand view of the famous cathedral at the top of the hill. Having been told that the trolley that passed by our hotel went very close to this historical edifice, we boarded it with assurance. Passing through the city and across the bridge,

we knew that we must be getting close to our destination.
Overeager, we got off the trolley only to find that it was
much too soon. So we began walking—interminably, so it
seemed as we wound round and round up the hill. When
we came to the place that we thought was close to the
cathedral, my husband said: "We're lost. I don't see even the
steeples any more. We must have taken the wrong way."
However, knowing we had been heading in the right
direction, we persisted in going on. Sure enough! We
rounded a corner, and there was the gate and beyond it the
cathedral. The buildings close by us had completely obliter-
ated the view of that which could be readily seen from afar.

So it is often in our praying. The wonder and reality
of the God to whom we may turn are lost in the pressure
of the needs about us. For enrichment in your prayer life,
first of all get the long look.

In James Weldon Johnson's book *God's Trombones* there
is a prayer of a worshipper for her pastor. One of the telling
petitions is:

> Lord God, this morning—
> Put his eye to the telescope of eternity,
> And let him look upon the paper walls of time.

In Psalm 95:6, 7, we have the call to worship which is the
synonym for adoration:

> O come, let us worship and bow down,
> let us kneel before the Lord, our Maker!
> For he is our God,
> and we are the people of his pasture,
> And the sheep of his hand.

"For the Lord is our Maker"—yes, ours, and the Maker of heaven and earth. Put into your own mouth the words of Ezra the priest, as they are recorded in Nehemiah 9:6:

> Thou art the Lord, thou alone;
> thou hast made heaven, the heaven of heavens,
> with all their host, the earth and all that is on it,
> the seas and all that is in them; and thou preservest
> all of them; and the host of heaven worships thee.

Pause, then, friend, as you enter the gate of prayer to consider to whom you are coming. Pause, and from the depth of your being, look up in adoration to say: "How great Thou art!" Read the 24th Psalm. Not only is the Lord our Maker; he is King. Exultantly the psalmist shouts:

> Lift up your heads, O gates!
> and be lifted up, O ancient doors!
> that the King of glory may come in! . . .
> Who is this King of glory?
> The Lord of hosts,
> he is the King of glory!

You who are fearful about the turbulent world in which we live, listen again to the trumpeted words of the seventh angel: "The kingdom of this world has become the kingdom of our Lord and of his Christ, and he shall reign forever and ever."

The God to whom you are coming is Maker, King, Judge. What a frightening thing this could be that he is our Judge, for this Judge needs no witnesses, but sees through us even to the murky depths of our subconscious. It is good for us to remember that we can hide nothing from him. In the gray religiosity of our day, the holiness of a just and righteous God is too often forgotten. When the merciless judgment of other people fells us, how great it is to remember that God is our final judge; that through faith in Christ, the judgment is one of mercy, not of our just desserts.

In John 5:24 we read: "Truly, truly, I say to you, he who hears my word and believes him who sent me, has eternal life; he does not come into judgment, but has passed from death to life."

Our forty-three-year-old nephew was struggling between life and death. He had been told that his illness was terminal. His uncle, who was also his pastor, came to his bedside. Until just the last months of his life, this young man had been so busy earning a living for his family that he had not been very faithful in church attendance, nor was he given to thinking too much about his soul. In desperation he turned to Uncle "Rube" and said: "What will it be like? How will God receive me? Have I done enough?" Can you imagine what it meant in a moment like this for the pastor by the authority of God's Word to be able to say: "Jack, it isn't what you have done, it is what Christ did for you that will really matter. *If you believe* that he is God's Son, and that he came into the world to save you from judgment for all the things you have not done, this is it. This is what is pleasing to God." As the pastor continued to share God's loving way to man, in Christ, a deep peace stole over the face of the sick young man.

There is a beautiful postscript to this story. Just three months before, Jack's wife, Marguerite, had preceded him in death. A lovely Christian woman, she had lived with cancer for ten years. When Jack was breathing his last, he opened his eyes. Those at the bedside witness to a golden light about his head as he exclaimed: "Marguerite, Marguerite!"

On the one hand we realize that it is a fearful thing to fall into the hands of a just God, on the other we remember his gracious provision for us in coming to pay the penalty of his judgment. Dimly the psalmist must have comprehended this when he burst into song:

> Let the heavens be glad, and let the earth rejoice;
> let the sea roar, and all that fills it;
> let the field exult, and everything in it;
> Then shall all the trees of the wood sing for joy
> before the Lord, for he comes,
> for he comes to judge the earth.
> He will judge the world with righteousness,
> and the peoples with his truth.

PSALM 96:11-13

How great thou art: Maker, King, Judge, Provider! Which one of us can even in a small way comprehend the providence of God? On a gray autumn day, a young lad from New England was leaving home to make his own way in the world. He felt somewhat lost and lonely and sad. Just when this mood almost overwhelmed him, he happened to see a waterfowl winging its way southward. To his mind there came the question: How did the bird know where to go? Who would take care of it? So it was that the boy, William Cullen Bryant, wrote the significant words:

He who from zone to zone
Guides through the boundless sky thy certain flight,
In the long way that I must tread alone,
Will lead my steps aright.

When we think of God's providence, often we think only of the spectacular ways in which he takes care of us. But his hand is constantly over us and his ear is always daily open to our cry. Do we worship and adore him for this?

The story is told of how Dr. John Witherspoon (signer of the Declaration of Independence) replied to the exciting tale of a neighbor. The man burst into Dr. Witherspoon's study and said, "You must join me in giving thanks to God for his extraordinary providence in saving my life. When I was driving from Rocky Hill the horse ran away and the buggy was smashed to pieces on the rocks, but I escaped unharmed!"

"Why," answered Dr. Witherspoon, "I can tell you a far more remarkable providence than that. I have driven over that road hundreds of times. My horse never ran away, my buggy was never smashed and I was never hurt."

How great thou art, who givest us each day our daily bread! Maker, King, Judge, Provider, Friend . . . . Can it possibly be that all of these are contained in one Person?

Humanly speaking we are aware of what it means to adore a friend. Do we stop to consider that the Almighty God, the Everlasting Father, the Prince of Peace, wants to be our friend? We kowtow to V.I.P.'s. We boast about little associations with them! Is my face red at this point! I remember the many times I have proudly shown the pictures where I am in the company of Mamie Eisenhower and Bess

Truman. How proud am I that Jesus Christ is my Friend?

What a Friend! He stays closer than a brother; he will never leave us or forsake us; he knows all about us and yet loves us. In his coming to earth to live and die for us, he proved the kind of a Friend he is. He suffered all kinds of ignominy and shame on our behalf. What adoration do we bring to such a Friend?

Do you know the joy of having him walking with you every day? Do you know the confidence of his presence no matter how difficult the situation in which you find yourself? Pause as you read and consider this Friend:

> What language shall I borrow
>   To thank thee, dearest friend,
> For this thy dying sorrow,
>   Thy pity without end?
> O make me thine forever,
>   And should I fainting be,
> Lord, let me never, never
>   Outlive my love to thee.

In the land of prayer, adoration is the first stop. Make it your daily, hourly experience. You cannot go grovelling through life if you take time to adore your Maker, Judge, Provider, and Friend.

Prayer

My heart lifts up in adoration, Jesus Christ, for the totality of your provision for me. My heart is too small to contain the wonder of your love. Oh, let the overflow bless the lives of others. Amen.

Travel Guides

1. How much of your prayer content is adoration?

2. Before you begin prayer time, pause in quietness to meditate on the One to whom you are praying. Think of him in each of the roles we have mentioned. Let your heart reach out to him.

3. When you see a flower, or hear a bird, or look into the uplifted face of a little child, pause to worship the One who created these wonders.

4. Make your own (yes—memorize) the words of such hymns as:

    "O God, how wonderful thou art"

    "How great thou art"

    "O what praises shall I render"

    "Praise to the Lord, the Almighty, the King of creation"

    Maybe you would like to use this prayer. A friend included it in a letter and I share it now.

A Deskside Prayer

Slow me down, Lord!

Ease the pounding of my heart by the quieting of my mind.

Steady my hurried pace with the vision of the eternal reach of time.

Give me, amidst the confusion of my day, the calmness of the everlasting hills.

Break the tensions of my nerves and muscles with the

soothing music of the singing streams that live in my memory.

Help me to know the magical, restoring power of sleep.

Teach me the art of taking minute vacations . . . or slow down to look at a flower, to chat with a friend, to pat a dog, to read a good book.

Remind me each day of the fable of the hare and the tortoise that I may know that the race is not always to the swift, that there is more to life than increasing its speed.

Let me look upward into the branches of the towering oak and know that it grew great and strong because it grew slowly and well.

Slow me down, Lord, and inspire me to send my roots deep into the soil of life's enduring values that I may grow toward the stars of my greater destiny.

We always pray in the name of Jesus. Amen.

ANON.

CHAPTER THREE

To the Land of Prayer:

Confession

In Psalm 51, by David, there is perhaps as dramatic and sincere a confession of sin as is to be found in all of the Bible. Search it out now and read it afresh. In the third verse the psalmist writes: "For I know my transgressions, and my sin is ever before me."

How many of us ever really "know" our transgressions? In his illustration of the mote and the beam, Jesus made it very clear how easy it is for us to see the fault in our brothers, and how difficult to be aware of the fault in ourselves. Psychologists tell us that the wrong we see in our fellowmen is often rooted in our own makeup. "Criticism is hidden resentment" is a statement from a contemporary book.

In the latter portion of Psalm 50 some common sins that we all commit are listed:

"You give your mouth free rein for evil, and your tongue frames deceit."

"You sit and speak against your brother; you slander your mother's son."

Here is a specific sin that is an obstacle to progress in the land of prayer.

19

Try a "playback" of your conversations this past week. Has your prayer been blocked because your small talk about others simply could not pass his censorship? What would Jesus do with a piece of gossip?

Or think for a moment about the things to which so much of your energy has been given. How would these stack up alongside of: "Seek first the kingdom of God and his righteousness"?

Take a look at the times when you have been in a "blue-funk." Isn't it plain that it is self-pity that pulled you into this swampy woods? The devil pushes faith out of the door to leave fear in charge. Underneath it all is that subtle question: "What is going to happen to *me?*" Sometimes self-pity is disguised even in the clothes of piety. Let us look closer at that which brings us so far short of what children of the king should be and clogs the channels of our communion with him.

In his book *Know Your Faith* Dr. Nils Ferre makes a telling distinction between our sins (plural) and the sin which so easily besets us. Might we not here be getting to the root of it all? He says: "Sin is what we are; sins are what we do. We sin most deeply by refusing to see ourselves as sinners."

Could it be that we are so little aware of the holiness of God to comprehend how removed we are by nature from him? Is it our natural instinct to obey him, or do we mostly consider ourselves? How often do we put on a pious front, chucking our rebellions into the subconscious? No wonder the sewer gasses of ill-will and resentment and hurt pride gather in the basement only to explode at some untoward time. Then we try in our own puny strength to contain these fearsome pressures. Who is sufficient to cope with these subterranean Freudian forces to which must be added our willfulness as over against God's will; our material well-being as over against our spiritual welfare? The battle is between the drum-major of our haughty ego and the servant with Christ-like humility. This is a work that only the Holy Spirit has the resources necessary to take over and give us the hope of victory.

Your journey into the land of prayer will be an utterly frustrating one unless you stop daily to look at yourself in the mirror of his Word, honestly facing your innate rebellion and acknowledging that only God can impower you to break free. Are you willing to confess that you have wanted to run your own life and that of your husband or wife and that of your children and your relatives—yes, even of your boss and your friends?

If you have come to the place where you are willing to acknowledge that you can't go it alone, that you don't have all the answers, that you have often gone your own way rather than God's—then he is ready for you, and eager to fling wide the gates for a prayer-powered life that will make living what he really means it to be—abundant!

The sacrifice acceptable to God is a broken spirit;
a broken and a contrite heart, O God, thou wilt not despise.

PSALM 51:17

Behold, thou desirest truth in the inward being;
therefore teach me wisdom in my secret heart.

PSALM 51:6

When you are alone, tell God what you feel deep within you. Talk to him aloud or write it on paper. It is harder for the devil to divert you if you make an overt act of this confession. Use the same means of confessing specific sins. Take a sharp look at them. Maybe never before have you dared to haul them out into the light and see them for what they are.

If these sins are against people, ask God for courage to make restitution with the wisdom that he will supply. Act on the impulses in this direction that the Holy Spirit will put into your heart. Each morning ask God for strength and grace not to repeat the things that grieve him.

Here there is a word of warning along the way. When you have given your sins to God, leave them there and don't grovel in them. In the book *Florence Allshorn* by Oldham there is a pertinent quote from this remarkable woman: "To keep looking at God and not at oneself and one's sins, this is the secret of spiritual growth." She quotes: "He hath brought me forth into a large place; he delivered me because he delighted in me." She continues: "How much higher a conception of God than the miserable sinner conception. It is more effective in every way. If you keep your face on the Father, he will help you to trample on your sins and keep climbing up. We can't do anything unless we have a spiritual passion greater than the sinful passions; this will have to be enormous!"

"Looking to Jesus, the author and finisher of our faith . . . ."

In one of our Bible classes, a friend gave a most strengthening witness. She is a woman who has had a real struggle.

Daily she faces a husband who wants to get rid of her because he is "in love" with someone else. Her confession, however, was about herself. She told of how, when confronting Christ anew in her life, she had prayerfully made a list of her faults as she saw them. "Believe me, there was quite a list," she said. "It astounded me when I saw it on paper." Then she told of how as she continued in the study of Scripture and prayer to better discern God's will for her life, there were days when she thought that she could almost cross some of them out, so effective had been the quiet work of the Holy Spirit. Then again—wham—her old nature would reassert itself and she would have to erase the crossing out.

Those of us who have seen the Christian maturing of this friend will attest to the validity of Christ's power in her life. It began when she with honesty acknowledged her sin, and asked for help.

A renowned physician tells the story of one of his arthritic patients who most of us would glibly say is hopelessly crippled. (Hopeless is the devil's favorite word and has no place in the vocabulary of a Christian.) An inner rebirth created a whole new perspective of life. Instead of folding up, she asked God for courage, patience, and strength for thirty minutes at a time. She admitted that she would need to lean entirely on him. What a victorious life, both physically and spiritually, she now is living—thirty minutes at a time.

A young man in the air force shared a wonderful bit of wisdom passed along by his Indian mother. She told him to ask the Great Spirit for wisdom and strength—but for two minutes at a time. "In this way," she said, "you will constantly be reminded of the One in whose hands your life is."

I do not care to see the distant scene;
One step enough for me.

Jesus Christ never had to walk the road of confession, for he is the Holy One, without sin. Knowing the frailty of our nature, he pointed the way for us, and makes it so very clear that only when we traverse the way marked Penitence are we really on our way Home. And besides, it will be with a new song on our lips, and a deep joy in our hearts!

So, in this matter of temptation and sin, we need to live moment by moment in his grace, and know that when we have confessed our sin and are truly sorry for having grieved him, then we have a new beginning. The fog that dimmed our sight of God is lifted, and the channels are open for his power.

Travel Guides

1. Is there something covered from a dear one that had better be confessed? Ask God for strength, and do it now.

2. Of what sins of thought have you been guilty? What does Jesus say about these?

3. With what is your greatest spiritual struggle? Worry, unbelief, doubt, critical attitudes toward others, wrong sense of values?

4. Do you know the joy of sins confessed and forgiven?

5. How ready are you to honestly forgive others: your family, your friends?

Prayer

Lord, you know me through and through. I want the searchlight of your Word to probe every corner of my being. In this stillness, now, Jesus, show me my sins and give me grace to confess them and loathe them. And give me grace to accept your wonderful forgiveness so dearly bought. Amen.

CHAPTER FOUR

To the Land of Prayer:

Thanksgiving

> It is good to give thanks to the Lord,
> to sing praises to thy name, O Most High;
> to declare thy steadfast love in the morning,
> and thy faithfulness by night,
> to the music of the lute and the harp,
> to the melody of the lyre.
> For thou, O Lord, hast made me glad by thy work;
> at the work of thy hands I sing for joy.
>
> PSALM 92:1-4

Have you ever traveled in New England in the autumn of the year, and lest I sound like a Chamber of Commerce folder, I'd better add: in sections of the Middle West, or the Pacific North West, or through the Alleghenies, or the Blue Ridge or Smoky Mountains, or anywhere where the seasons change and God has enriched the land with beautiful trees? Can you call to mind the exuberance of heart, mind, yes, and body, as one turn of the road reveals beauty more breathtaking than the preceding one? It seems as if all nature in this harvest time of the year is clapping its hands and praising its Creator. Aren't you moved at this sight to want to

27

join in, to shout your gratitude for the wonder of God and join all living things in his praise? Or in our multi-gadgeted world, with its variegated neon lights, amidst the tinsel and trappings of contemporary living, have we lost the gift of gratitude? When did you last really follow this road in the land of prayer?

When the psalmist says: "It is good to give thanks to the Lord," he isn't just speaking pious phrases. It is a good exercise for our whole being. It cleanses us of the sourness of gripes, of the stench of complaint, of the mildew of discouragement. Giving thanks does for the mind what cleaning house does for your home when you have washed every nook and cranny and cleaned every cupboard and closet. There is a fresh new beginning-again feeling that is the sweetest kind of fragrance. Perfume manufacturers have devised all kinds of fantastic names for their various brands to lure the gullible buyer. But there is nothing that can even match thanksgiving perfume. Its fragrance lingers long after the person's presence has passed, and its deposit in the mind is more potent and lasting than the sachet bags that permeate our linens with their essence.

Not only does a thankful spirit bless other people, but it is a wonderful producer of mental health. Here is where the body is affected too, for the attitudes of the mind can create and destroy chemicals that keep the bodily machinery in good running order. Giving thanks is the balm of Gilead for one's whole being: it relaxes the tension as we recount our God-given resources and their adequacy for any and every exigency as we acknowledge God's providential love. To give thanks is a splendid rule of health.

More than this, it focuses our eyes on our life's goal and gives us perspective. Why were Paul the apostle and his co-laborer Silas able to sing in prison, and at midnight besides? Did their flogged and bleeding bodies actually feel so pain-free as to make them joyous? Was it because being man-acled and bound and behind bars was a situation to be de-sired? Why do they praise God instead of moaning and clenching their teeth? Paul could sing at midnight because he could view the present situation in the light of the goals of God's kingdom. The Christ within him rose to change the whole experience from one of physical torture to one that could be used to praise God and witness to the power of the resurrected Christ. In your darkest moments, try praising and thanking God, and recounting his hand in your life in the past, and this miracle will happen to you too. It has hap-pened to us again and again.

When one of our children was very ill, and his fragile house of life seemed utterly broken, there came to us, as if spoken by the Lord in person, the words Paul wrote to the Philippians: "Have no anxiety in anything, but in everything with praise and thanksgiving . . . . " We began recounting all the times the Lord had so wonderfully shown his love to us, his amazing goodness in the life of the sick child, and the heavy load was lifted from our hearts.

Jesus led the way on the thanksgiving road. He thanked God that he had hidden things from the wise and prudent and revealed them unto babes. In the Lord's Supper, when he had given thanks, he broke the bread and took the cup. In the inn at the end of the Emmaus Road, it was in the giving of thanks that he was recognized. When he broke the loaves and the fishes he gave thanks. Many of the great passages of the Bible center around thanksgiving. Search them out for yourself.

In his book *The Heavenly Father,* Dr. Thielicke tells of a friend who witnesses to the power of praise in his horrible experiences of the World War of the forties. The tremendous witness that his calm composure gave inspired peace and comfort in those around him. He was in a place where there were constant bombings and people panicked with fear. He tells of how, in the most frightful air raids, he stopped calling upon God and only continued to praise him. This lifted him above the ghastly moments when the bombs were falling. He was able to fix his eyes on the eternity of God, and in the light of this perspective, the few anguished seconds seemed not too relevant. His thoughts were able to rise above the five alarms. Someone has aptly said: "I can't live the present victoriously unless I believe in the future gloriously."

I like the ingenuity of the workman who had been given an extra tip, and so thought he'd surprise Miranda by buying a steak. Ordinarily these folks were "hamburger" people. He carried the precious meat in his hand by the string which held its wrapping, and whistled as he walked along, his arm swinging the package. Now this fellow had the fine habit of saying, no matter what happened, "Praise the Lord." Even when he might accidentally hit his thumb while hammering, he would say, "Praise the Lord." In the course of his homeward journey, a hound scented the meat, and before the man could protect it the dog had escaped with the prize package. A friend who had observed the catastrophe said: "Now, Sam! Surely you'll not say, 'Praise the Lord!'"

"Yessir," said Sam. "I now say, 'Praise the Lord' because I still have my appetite!"

We heard a beautiful witness from a man who thanked God even for his defeat. His wife, in speaking of some of the executives of the company for which he worked, said: "My husband should have been one of them! He has earned it over and over again!" Then this fine Christian gentleman said: "But dear, I wouldn't have had the Christian experience I've had. Maybe I wouldn't have been willing to serve on the church council; maybe I wouldn't have taken time to know the rich experience of prayer. God has filled my life with greater blessings."

If you knew the man, you'd know this wasn't "sour grapes." Whereas others have pouted and complained because they felt they had been passed by on the promotion line, this Christian had matured to where he could thank God for it, because spiritual good had come.

There is yet another facet to this experience that we should mention. It is a wonderful thing to say thank you to our loved ones and our friends. How eager we are, as we train our children, to develop this grace. Yet very often in our homes, where the real training ground is, we are very slow to acknowledge gratitude to those closest to us for the everyday things that are so quickly taken for granted. When did you last say thank you to those closest to you?

Wives, to your husbands for their providence and support. Husbands, to your wives for making *home* (that drawer full of clean shirts, that fresh bed for your weary body, that tastefully prepared meal for your nourishment and refreshment).

Children, to your parents for their loving care and concern and their discipline.

Parents, to your children for the joy of them and what they have brought to your lives.

Employer, to your subordinates who make it possible for your business to flourish.

Employee, to your boss for the opportunities that are yours in your work.

Pupil, to your teacher for the privilege of learning.

Teacher, to your pupil for cooperation and helpfulness.

Well, the list is endless. Today you can bless somebody's life by saying thank you, and at the same time you will be blessing your own.

In Colossians 3:17 we read: "And whatever you do in word or deed, do everything in the name of the Lord Jesus, giving *thanks* to God the Father through him."

Travel Guides

1. Write down the things in your life for which you thank God. (In a circle of friends treat yourselves to an experience by having each share his most grateful moment.)

2. Pause at the throne of grace to give this list to God.

3. Search your heart for the areas of neglected gratitude in your human relations. Do something about these as God reveals them. (Write a letter, make a telephone call, bake a cake and deliver it. If you're a man, buy a flower as

your outward symbol.) But *act* on the God-given impulse of gratitude.

Thanksgiving Prayer

Thank you, Jesus Christ, for the wonder of your love. Thank you for revealing the Father. Thank you for the prodding of the Holy Spirit that shows me my thankless-ness. Thank you that I may be a channel of gratitude in the lives of others. For your Word, for the privilege of prayer, for a life to live in your love; for all these, thank you, Lord. Amen.

CHAPTER FIVE

To the Land of Prayer:

Supplication

"First of all, then, I urge that supplications, prayers, inter-cessions, and thanksgivings be made for all men, for kings and all who are in high positions, that we may lead a quiet and peaceable life, godly and respectful in every way. This is good, and it is acceptable in the sight of God our Savior, who desires all men to be saved and to come to the knowl-edge of the truth" (1 Timothy 2:1-4).

"Is any among you suffering? Let him pray. Is any cheer-ful? Let him sing praise. Is any among you sick? Let him call for the elders of the church, and let them pray over him, anointing him with oil in the name of the Lord; and the prayer of faith will save the sick man, and the Lord will raise him up; and if he has committed sins, he will be for-given" (James 5:13-15).

Add your own favorite Scripture call to prayer. The Bible is full of them. God has entreated us countless times to come to him with our petitions and our needs. He loves to have his children call upon him in faith. Why don't we?

Look at the world in which we live. What a mess! Name any section of it, and immediately there is conjured up a place of tension, a trouble spot, angry people. How many of us Christians really lift our harried leaders to God in prayer? Yet many grumble and complain about their leadership! In his letter to young Timothy, in which he is offering counsel to the young man concerning the training of the leaders of the young church, the Apostle Paul specifically enjoins such supplications. Were the leaders in those days basically any different from the ones we have now?

Let us momentarily get the background of this writing. There were no church buildings in those first centuries, but in a thriving city like Ephesus, where Timothy had been left in charge, the church was meeting in hundreds of homes and so needed hundreds of leaders. These were called elders and bishops. There were no schools of theology at which they might be trained. Timothy's job was to select the most likely converts and school them in the truths which the Apostle Paul had taught them when he was there. These, then, were to be the leaders in the church which met in these homes. This call to prayer was one of the first matters that the apostle emphasizes in his letter of instruction. How desperately we need to give ear to it in our churches today! Show me the church that has an alive, faithful, glowing prayer life, and I'll guarantee that here will be a church that is serving in this present age. Show me the person whose world concern is a constant matter of prayer, and I'll warrant you that he is one who is doing something about the situations that seem hopeless. Frank Laubach coined the term "a war of amazing kindness." How about the amazing war we Christians can fight with the simple weapon of prayer? Praying people can indeed change not only the course of a nation, but of a world.

How can you know for whom to pray? Some people use prayer lists. Yet even some of these very earnest folk have commented on how these can grow stale. How do you know when to take a person off your prayer list, lest the latter become an endless and tedious repetition of mere names?

Dr. George S. Stewart, in his book *The Lower Levels of Prayer,* makes a practical and helpful suggestion. As you sit quietly before the Lord, let those names that come to you be the ones that you write down for the beginning of your list. This should not be pressed into a hunt for names. As you wait upon the Lord expectantly, trust his Spirit to guide you. The names will be given. Some of these may even be personally distasteful to you, but this is just an invitation to a real adventure in prayer living. Very likely God will consequently put it upon your heart to *do* something for them which can then remove the distaste.

To really give yourself to persisting prayer is dangerous. There have been times in my life when I have come to prayer with hurt feelings, hoping to find the balm that my wounded pride needed (so I thought). Instead God has lifted me from my needs with the compulsion to go to the one in question and ask his forgiveness for my part in the misunderstanding. This is exactly the opposite of what I had expected when I went to my knees; I had thought God would send him to me asking me to forgive him. This is a particular miracle when the other party happens to be your husband or your wife. What an experience of the divine alchemy! You'll recognize it as you find yourself doing something that you never expected to do.

Another helpful suggestion that Dr. Stewart makes is that one name suggests others. Suppose you are praying for someone fighting alcoholism; as you lift this person to God, several others with the same problem may come to your mind. So it can be that parents praying for a wayward son at the same time can be praying for all wayward sons. Certainly their John will have the center of their prayer, but gathered around him will be many others with similar needs.

So it is when you pray for somebody who is sorrowing. In his world-inclusive heart, God is reminded of the sorrowing around the world, and will call to your mind, too, others to be included. Isn't God wonderful? That he deigns to use us as his channels is something that I cannot comprehend, but can only praise him for. Surely this kind of praying is like the old illustration of the pebble dropped into a pond, which, troubling the water at a given point, sends its ever-widening circles on and out until they reach the other shores.

There is a danger in trying to cover too much territory in your prayers, so that your involvement in them becomes too thin. This is the great weakness of our age in so many matters. To pray in depth means to really give yourself to the person or problem. Humanly speaking, you cannot do this with too many at a time. Therefore it is advisable to have different times in which to remember people and situations.

Not long ago we were going through the bazaar at Beirut. The streets were crowded with people going in different directions. What a cross-section of humanity! The obviously wealthy were rubbing elbows with the beggars in their rags. Here were men and women in such attire as to inspire one to call them Abraham and Sarah. It was as if the centuries had been rolled back. In the same streets were women attired in the latest Parisian fashions. The former were seeking their simple daily fare in the fruit and vegetable market; the latter, bargaining in the gold "suk." Little children underfoot stretched out dirty hands pleading: "Baksheesh." Yesterday, today, and tomorrow; leanness, affluence, and need—everywhere people, and behind these unseen millions more—so many of them strangers to the Savior, the one hope of the world.

That same day in the portion of the Bible which we turned to for our study was the well-known account of Jesus feeding the five thousand. It was as if God gave me this passage for this particular day. Had I not come to my hotel room thinking: "What ever is going to happen to all these people? How are they to learn about Jesus, their Savior and Friend?" The miracle of the multiplication of the loaves and fishes I had read hundreds of times, but this day it spoke to me in a very special way. I was the modern disciple saying to Jesus in a spiritual sense: "Our feeble efforts, Lord, what are these among so many?" The Lord's answer was as of old: "Bring them to me." I arose from my knees, knowing anew that the multiplying was his province; mine was to bring what I had to him—and to trust him.

In the book *Angel at Her Shoulder,* a biography of that remarkable little woman, Lillian Dickson, of Taiwan, there is told the story of how she came home one day and said: "We must do something about the tubercular people. There are thousands of them getting no care whatsoever!" To which her friend, groaning, replied: "You can't start that, too. You already have more projects going than seem humanly possible. This one is overwhelming. It would be like trying to empty the ocean with a teacup." "That may well be," was the reply of this intrepid woman, "but as a Christian I must use the teacup."

In our prayers of intercession and supplication, our little "lunches" may seem very insignificant. But the Lord stands ready to do it again: feed the multitude with one person's dedication of what he has. He will use you to become the answer.

In the fourth chapter of Exodus, Moses has quite an argument with God because Moses felt so inadequate. Then God said to him, "What is that in your hand?" "A rod," Moses replied. Then the Lord told him to cast it down, and as he did, it became a serpent. Moses was frightened and fled from it. The Lord told him to take it up by the tail. As Moses did this, it became a rod in his hand.

What is in *your* hand?

God is asking us to so grow in faith, that as we give our hearts and gifts to him, great things will happen. Just try him once and see for yourself!

It may be helpful for a moment to think in terms of a possible classification of prayers, remembering, however, that there is only one basic division: those we know are in the will of Christ, and those about whom we must plead for his will to be shown. To pray for a soul to be redeemed certainly does not have to have appendaged to it, "If it be thy will." Scripture clearly states that God wants all men to be saved; that God so loved the *world*. So when you are praying for someone's soul, you know you are in the will of God, and what you are asking is pleasing to him. By the same token, too, since sickness is in the world only because of sin, because of man's disobedience to God, you can pray for anyone's wholeness with the same confidence. These are prayers that Scripture assures us are in the will of God.

On the other hand, when you are praying about things pertaining to your material life: your job, your marriage, your opportunities (or those of your loved ones), surely you would want to pray specifically for God's will to be revealed and done, even though it might be quite contrary to your human desires. It really boils down to your releasing all that you have and are into the wonderful arms of God, your heavenly Father, who will do more for you than you can ever ask or think. According to the measure of your faith.

There is another kind of prayer that we may participate in and hardly be aware of: ejaculatory prayers and prayers of benediction. These are like the air we breathe. Our daughter wrote and spoke of the beauty of Mount Kilimanjaro in Africa during the various times of the day and night. When the purple shadows of evening fall it is cloaked in a star-studded majesty; the first blush of dawn brushes the snow-covered crest with delicate pink; and then when the sun arises and lifts the veils, there it is in its dazzling white-crowned splendor against the azure sky. Then she said, "My heart cries out in each mood: 'How great thou art!'"

How vividly I remember the times when I was hanging out clothes in our back yard in Washington, when ejaculatory prayers of praise would call out from my lips. We had a climbing yellow rosebush that in the spring of the year was covered with voluptuous bursts of gold. When a cardinal made this vine his momentary resting place, the glory of the picture was too much to contain. "O God, how beautiful! Thank you, thank you!" would rush to my lips.

Or again in a crowded airport, when my attention would be called to some act of kindness one traveler was showing to another, inaudibly there would come: "Bless you. God bless you!"

What a land for our journeying—Supplication Street in the Land of Prayer! Following the Master will mean your being led here so constantly, as to make this land your native land.

Such journeying becomes a foretaste of eternity.

How well-traveled are you? These are the sign posts:

Adoration
Confession
Thanksgiving
Supplication

From such journeyings come the Acts of the Apostles!

Not always are the answers to our supplications as dramatic as the following one. But when there is a "oneness" of intense desire in the will of the Lord, the answer is on the way!

In Washington, D.C., the Department of the Army has made available the following incident. A little group of U.S. "G.I.'s" were cornered on an island of the South Seas that differed in its geography from the rest of them. This one was dry and rocky.

Moreover, they were cut off from their supplies and had not the slightest idea where they were. They didn't dare leave their foxholes lest they should become an immediate target for the enemy. The tropical heat began to tell on their parched bodies and they were getting more and more desperate.

With each passing day their thirst drove them to the edge of madness and their fevered eyes conjured up great surrounding lakes to taunt them. Then they prayed! With intense concentration they joined their prayers with the halting words of the one who was their spokesman to God.

He prayed, "God, give us water. If Moses could call on you in the past and strike a rock and bring forth water, you have the power today to perform another miracle like that for us, now! O God, hear our prayer. We must have water!"

Within a minute after the prayer, one of the Japanese shells fell only a few feet away and blasted open the rock where it fell. In the open hole made in the rocky terrain an underground spring was opened. From out of it gushed clear, cool water. It flowed directly to the foxhole where the men were hiding, and they lived to share this remarkable answer to prayer.

Do you sin—by not praying?

Travel Guides

1. Is your prayer experience joyful? Is it a growing experience?

2. Share with someone this week a prayer experience that will strengthen their faith.

3. Search the Scriptures for power-packed promises.

4. Claim them in whatever area of distress or need or gratitude you may find yourself.

5. Take inventory of your faith.

Prayer

We confess, O Lord, that we have not because we ask not; and then we ask amiss. Jesus, teach us to pray, that the powers of eternal love may be released in our individual lives and in all the world. Amen.

CHAPTER SIX

To God's House

Following Jesus, we will find ourselves unavoidably led to one place, the house of God. Read Luke 4:14-30. In verse 14: "He taught in their synagogues ... " and in 16: " ... so he came to Nazareth where he had been brought up; and he went to the synagogue, as his custom was, on the sabbath day." In the second chapter of Luke you will find him as a twelve-year-old boy responding to his mother's: "Your father and I have been looking for you anxiously" with: "How is it that you sought me? Did you not know that I must be in my Father's house?"

There is another scene from the life of our Lord concerning the Temple. This experience followed the Palm Sunday one. You remember how, coming to the Temple, he found petty bartering and the buying and selling of pigeons as well as the maneuvering of the money-changers. Having driven them out, he began to teach them with the words: "My house shall be called a house of prayer for all nations" (Mark 11:15-17).

From one of our youth camps was reported the following experience: In a group discussing the value of worship was

45

a scruffy-haired boy, a freshman in high school. "Isn't the church," the moderator suggested, "and worship, just a valueless form that we go through, and this whole thing of shared public faith kind of phony?" "No, it isn't," said the boy. "Well, why? What makes it worth anything?" he was pushed to answer. "Well," was the lad's response, "it helped me."

One of the great pulpiteers of our day tells of his first conscious awareness of the presence of God. He was eight years old. On this particular Sunday it seemed the harassments at home had been particularly aggravating. His mother was all in a knot as they breathlessly made their way into church. Then she bowed her head in prayer. The lad at her side could physically feel the release of his mother's distraught spirit into the keeping of her loving heavenly Father. He took a peek at her face, and what he saw there made him know that he was in the presence of something very holy.

Let's take a look at some of the attitudes that spoil the worship experience. I wonder what it would be like if our minds could be read as we take our places in the pew. Here is Mr. Johnson. He really wanted to sleep this morning, but his wife nagged so that he thought he might just as well give in and go. He wishes that he might find an inconspicuous place where he can take a little nap. Even that has its drawback, because his wife's elbow is plenty sharp when she nudges him.

There is Mr. Brown, the self-termed intellectual, who is there to see what sport he can have in punching holes in the logic of the preacher's sermon. He shifts from one foot to the other during the hymn singing, and fingers through the hymnal during the prayer, and lifts a lip-curled countenance to the pulpit when the preaching is about to begin.

Or there is the heresy-hunter, who is there with his pharisaical fine comb to search out any possible deviations from his rigid way of thinking or his fixed interpretation of the Word.

We must not leave out Mrs. Fashion Plate. Where better, to this many people, could one parade one's finery? Coming a little late is always helpful.

Friend, can you imagine the grace of God that it takes to face a congregation like this, and love them, and *believe* that God's Word will not return void? How desperately the man in the pulpit needs our prayers! And lest the picture be all black, let us remember that in every congregation there are those earnest souls who are the salt about which Jesus spoke. The Holy Spirit would ask of each of us: What is our attitude in church?

There is a step, prior to our arriving in the sanctuary, that we should consider. How regularly do you attend worship services? In your home is this one of those decisions that has to be made anew each week? Or is there the sense of sturdy dependability in the unquestioned practice that when Sunday comes, whatever else we may plan, this is what we will do; this time is set aside for our corporate worship of God. How grateful I am to parents who joyously set this pattern for their children!

At a youth retreat in Arabia, the discussion was on the times in our lives when we were most blessed—the really happiest times. One of the lovely young teen-agers sought out the leader afterwards and said: "Do you know when the

happiest time of all is in my life? It is when our whole
family is together in church."

Do you know the joy of finding your place in God's house,
putting aside all the frets and concerns of the tempestuous
world in which you live and losing yourself to God in
prayer? Have you had the experience of a heavy weight
being lifted from your soul as you met him in the appointed place and gave your burden to him?

What mistaken notions we often have about church worship. Erroneously, we measure the success or failure of it
largely by the power and eloquence of the preacher. How
many people flit from one church to another, sampling the
fare, seeking the one that is the most palatable. No matter
what the trappings of any service, no matter what the gifts
(or lack of them) might be the portion of the preacher, a
sincere worshipper can meet his God at the appointed time
of prayer and in the appointed place. God has given his
promise. Besides, you can contagiously convey the ecstasy of
your experience to others until they know the joy of a meeting with God, face to face.

Most congregations have never really laid hold of what
prayer in the pew can mean to power in the pulpit. Why not
try getting to church fifteen minutes early, quietly taking
your place, and giving yourself in earnest prayer for the
minister and the service? Every Sabbath would become a
Pentecost.

Dr. Clarence Cranford of Calvary Baptist Church in
Washington, D.C., relates an experience he had one Sunday
morning. He thought he had prepared a pretty good sermon,
but discovered at his first service that it didn't "take." Before the second service, he went to one of his parishioners

whom he knew to be faithful in prayer and said: "Mrs. Jones, something was wrong in that service this morning. Will you do me a favor? Will you be in prayer this next service that I'll permit the Holy Spirit to use me?" Fire fell at the second service, so the pastor went to his friend afterwards to thank her for her prayer support. "There were twelve of us praying," she responded. "We knew the Lord would use you."

How does one best prepare for the journey to God's house? Here is where my beloved parents set a worship pattern for us children. Every Saturday evening we shared together at family devotions the Gospel text for the next day. This was in all simplicity good ground-breaking to precede the sowing of the Word from the pulpit. Then we joined in prayer for the one who was to break the bread on the morrow. This was a part of our being able to say sincerely on Sunday: "I was glad when they said unto me, 'Let us go into the house of the Lord.'"

We have mentioned the joy of coming to church early to pray. Some of my richest moments have been such experiences. To pray for each person as he comes to worship; to remember the choir, the acolytes, the ushers, the organist, as well as the pastor, in prayer—this is to know something of the promised joy of the "Communion of Saints, the Holy Christian Church."

Nor does it end in the pew. After the service God will make your heart sensitive to the lonely people that might be there, or the stranger in your midst. You will make come alive again that word that characterized the early church: koinonia — fellowship, the fellowship of the concerned. Maybe you will ask someone home to dinner or make an appointment to meet them next week or offer to call for them to bring them to Bible study. Lots of things can happen to the person who has been praying in church. Something should happen to each one of us when we meet our Lord in his appointed place. Does it happen to you?

> Day of God, so sweet and fair,
> Call us now to praise and prayer,
> Gift of God to mortals given;
> Foretaste of the joy of heaven.
>
> When the week of labor ends,
> And the peace of God descends,
> O how sweet it is to meet
> At the holy Savior's feet.

Travel Guides

1. What is your attitude about church-going? Can you honestly make your own the words of Psalm 26:8?
2. Would a stranger stepping into your worship service be made aware of the love of Christ there?
3. What carry-over into your daily life is there of what you have received at the service?
4. How does the Christian fellowship evidence itself through the week?

Prayer

Forgive me, Lord, the times I have gone to your house with the wrong attitude. Help me to bring to each service such an expectant faith as to invite a Pentecost. Begin the outpouring of your Spirit on me! Amen.

CHAPTER SEVEN

Into People's Lives

If the heart and mind will follow Jesus, there is no question where the feet will go and what the hands will do. An inner compulsion of love will direct in no uncertain way. What an adventure—to follow Jesus into the lives of people! Every day has a prospect.

Today, if you will earnestly seek him out, he will put upon your heart someone who needs Christ's love channeled through you. It may be through the simplest means: a telephone call where the content has a word of faith; a letter with its witness to someone that there are those that care; a visit to some chronic invalid or some lonely person, or some forgotten aged one. Maybe his voice will guide you to do something closer to home than all these. It could be to do some loving little extra thoughtfulness for your husband, wife, children, parents, or any of your relatives.

Often, in our looking far afield for someone to serve, we overlook the needs of those immediately about us. If we are going to follow the commands of Jesus, we will do both.

There were times in his ministry when the Lord seemed almost brusque to his family. It was only when his family seemed to interfere with his Father's business that this was true. How lovingly did he not provide for Mary at the cross, and could it not well have been that those thirty years in Nazareth were to take care of her and the younger children until the latter could step up and help, since Joseph, the father, had died? Then, too, was there ever a time when anyone in need came to him and was turned away? Did the words, "I'm too busy," ever fall from Jesus' lips when there were those who needed him? Could it be that we could get so involved in studying our Bibles about him that we do not have time to follow him?

Yes, he was concerned about those immediately about him, but were not all his pronouncements inclusive of the world? When he looked to the whitening harvest, there was his all-embracing yearning expressed; when he spoke of other sheep "that are not of this fold," he must have had in mind the Gentile people; when he broke down one barrier after the other of race and tradition and intellect and position and sex, he was saying to all the world: "I have come to save *you* and to give you abundant life here and now and forever!" His "Go into all the world . . . " command wraps it all up.

But there is more to service than an area to be covered. There is a quality that the Lord insisted was very essential.

In John 12:26, we read his words: "If any one serves me, he must follow me; and where I am, there will my servant be also; if any one serves me, the Father will honor him." Surely the words to couple with these are some of the best known ones of our Lord, so often quoted and so little followed! "I was hungry and you gave me food; I was thirsty and you gave me drink; I was a stranger and you welcomed me; I was naked and you clothed me; I was sick and you visited me; I was in prison and you came to me." Anyone bored? Here is a pattern for living that will cut such a rich cloth as to be a blessing for all eternity. Let's try to spell it out, practically, in our daily lives.

We had better go to this same section of John for some directives as to preparation. In the two preceding verses of the one we have read is the cue. The Lord speaks of the necessity of a grain of wheat falling into the ground and dying before it can bring forth fruit, and in the ensuing explanation he says (the New English translation puts this clearly): "The man who loves himself is lost, but he who hates himself in this world will be kept safe for eternal life." If you are to follow Jesus in the path of service, it can't be at your own convenience or according to your pleasure. Nor can it always be the kind of work you choose to do. It might even be a task that repels you.

When he took a towel and washed his disciples' feet, he was doing a task that not even a servant was asked to do in those days. Only a slave performed this menial service. Do you have any idea what a shock this must have been to his disciples? He, their Master, taking the place of a slave! You know he wasn't pulling any grandstand dramatics! He was simply setting the pattern for those who loved him to follow. I have heard "Christian" women say: "Well, I consider that beneath me. Can't we hire someone to do it?" Or again: "What do we pay taxes for? Aren't there social workers hired to do these jobs?" Others may not have said it, but their actions witnessed to the fact that this was the way they felt.

The late Lydia Langer, wife of the senator from North

Dakota, walked in our midst as an example of what it means to follow Christ in this respect. Though she had hired help to clean her own home, as a member of the Altar Guild she reported regularly with pail and brush to help scrub the altar and to keep the Lord's house clean and beautiful. She gave great joy to the aged and often entertained them in her home. She visited the lonely international students who were hospitalized and befriended them in every kind of way. All of this was done very quietly and without any fanfare.

In her terminal illness, one day she turned to her pastor and said: "You know, Pastor, I've flavored life in many ways. I've been in the social whirl of New York and Washington and have gone to bed 'hungry.' It is only since I have been confronted with the reality of Christ in my life that I have begun to live."

We were privileged to share with this gracious lady her last days on earth. The beauty and serenity of spirit with which she made her way *home* is unforgettable. For her, as for the apostle, "To live was Christ, and to die, gain."

Dr. William Barclay says that there were three things that Jesus was saying at this point: (1) Only by death comes life. It is only when you are willing to bury your personal aims and plans and be open to the guidance of God, that he can use you. (2) Only by spending life do we retain it. For how long can you keep anything of this world that you gather? What are the richest memories of your life? Where is the place "where neither moth nor rust corrupt and where thieves do not break through and steal"? (3) Only by service comes greatness. Something of this spirit is illustrated by the English woman who became very well known as a Salvation Army worker in Liverpool. When she became old, she moved to London to retire. Then came the war and the war raids, and even though her house was poor, word went around that it was particularly safe. She felt that she must do something about it. So she got together a simple first-aid box and put up a sign in her window: "If you need help, knock here."

What a contrast this is to those of us who wear an invisible sign: "Don't bother me. I have enough trouble of my own." All the while the major part of our own solution is in our rejection of thinking about ourselves to be helpful to others. We won't get ourselves off our hands in any other way.

Yes, this lap of our journey, to follow Jesus in the walk of service, requires this costly preparation: so yielding ourselves to his will that we are willing to say: "Lord, my time, my energies, my talent, my means, are at your disposal. I'll go where you want me to go, day by day." Then adventure lies ahead!

Travel Guides

1. What is my attitude toward life and what should happen to me?

2. What is my attitude toward other people? Are there those to whom I feel superior?

3. Am I willing to do only certain kinds of things or am I flexible enough to try new patterns if God should so lead?

4. Am I willing to be inconvenienced to be of service to someone else, even to the changing of my personal plans?

5. Do I have the daring to open myself daily to the paths of service which he would have me walk?

Prayer

I've been pretty sleazy, Lord, in my concern for my fellowmen and in trying to be the channel for your love in other people's lives. Please forgive me and alert me to the opportunity there is for me today, where I am, and with what you have given me. Let me be still enough to be aware of your gentle nudgings, and then give me grace to act upon them. Of myself, I'm utterly helpless; but by your grace, anything can happen! Begin with me. Amen.

CHAPTER EIGHT

Into the Lives of the Hungry and Thirsty

In following our Master into other people's lives, we find there are various needs that present themselves. In the succeeding chapters we shall deal with some of these more specifically. We ask the question: How concerned is the Lord with our physical needs?

In a discussion group in our church in Washington, one of the G.I.'s said: "I can't 'buy' that God cares about every little thing that happens to us. He is too majestic and great for that. He controls the whole universe. How can he be concerned about the small everyday details of the life of little me?"

During his Washington stay, the Lord put his hand on this young man's life and directed him to the seminary. This was quite a challenge, for he was married and had a little son. However, he found evening work and a Sunday preaching opportunity came his way. We treasure the letter he sent later in the year!

"You know," he said, "I used to ridicule the idea that God could be concerned about each detail of our lives. We want to confess that we now know that this is true. We are constantly amazed at his providence, which, every time when we think we have reached a blank wall, opens up a way."

God cares about us. He wants us to be concerned about the total needs of others. Dr. Martin Luther so succinctly said: "By this shall all men know whether or not the birth of Christ is effective in you: how you take upon yourself the need of your neighbor."

Read again the story of the feeding of the four thousand as it is recorded in Matthew 15:32-38. Listen to Jesus' words: "I have compassion on the crowd . . . I am unwilling to send them away hungry . . . "

There is nothing that haunts me quite as much as what we experienced in Al Khobar, an Arab town about five miles from Dhahran, where we lived. You never walk down the street or come out of a store but what you are accosted by an Arab woman in her black abba. Through the veil that covers her face, you see her imploring eyes and you are aware of her outstretched hand for "baksheesh." Often, the outstretched hand of the whimpering little one in her arms is cleverly substituted. Maybe the extended hand is that of a blind man, led by a ragged little boy!

During the fast period of Ramadan one is surrounded on all sides by these poor people with their appealing hands. According to the Muslim religion, there is a special blessing for those who share with the poor at this time. In fact, it is a stewardship required of you. Yet we know that this is not the answer. Many people piously drop their "girsch" in these people's palms as a soporific to their conscience. In this way they excuse themselves from putting into long-term action any program that would provide gainful labor for these folks to give them a sense of person-hood and respectability, making begging unnecessary.

Lest we pharisaically look with disdain at our Arab neighbors at this point, let us be honest enough to admit that there are plenty of us in America who do the same. Had we been more concerned about equal job opportunities, education, and housing for our Negro neighbors, we would not be having the riots in United States today.

This question arises: Is there any real substitute for personal concern? Certainly if a hungry person comes to my door, I give him food. But his basic problem is still there. Furthermore, back there in Khobar, it would be impossible for me to give even a little to all who hold out their hands. Nor is it always simple to detect real need. Sometimes you would see pearls and even 18 carat bangles on the outstretched arms. What to do!

An Icelandic friend who worked at the airport, and whose tender heart just couldn't pass them by, devised a way to ease his conscience. He went to the local bakery, and bought up small loaves of their inexpensive bread. These he carried with him, and when a palm was extended he placed one of these in it. This gave him a good deal of satisfaction. Yet, how much of the problem did it solve? What lasting contribution had been made to curing poverty?

This extreme situation is somewhat removed from most of us. The problem, however, should be the concern of every Christian everywhere. Certainly it is true that in recent times we have been made more aware of conditions that exist in our own country that should arouse our concerted efforts to alleviate. I, for one, am grateful for the stimulus of the President's campaign against poverty. We cannot be content to end here. As citizens of the world we should be sensitive to every area of need, and we should encourage every venture of honest sharing. If we are to follow Jesus, there is no escape from this.

There have been times when I have heard Americans say: "Why should we feed the whole world? What do we get for it but ignominy and abuse?" Certainly the methods used haven't always been the best, and often the motives are mixed in our sharing programs. Sometimes the personnel involved has been the key to inefficiency and mismanagement. But God have pity on our souls if we don't keep trying to find the best way possible to share with the hungry everywhere! We need to share our surpluses as an immediate aid, but much more than this, we need to share our skills, our scientific know-how, our concern, and our love. *We are writing our own death sentences if we do not!* You cannot turn your back on need and not know inner decay.

So where does this leave you? There is the twofold prong! First, in your neighborhood, in your community, you as a Christian citizen should make it your business to be aware of areas of need and bring what remedy you can to them, and enlist others to do the same. Second, you should be informed of those world programs that are endeavoring to produce food for the hungry, and you should make your voice heard in government, in civic organizations, in whatever openings God may lead you to, that the much may be shared with those who have so little. You bring to this interest your Christian concern, and trust God for the rest.

There is another hunger that is more important than the first, although it is difficult to divorce the two of them. The second hunger is the hunger of the heart. The only food

that can satisfy this is love. Here the symptoms are so subtle. Maybe a son is rebellious and at odds with everyone as
well as with himself. Deep down within him, without his
even knowing it, he may have the feeling that he isn't really
loved. He may come from a home where every material
benefit is his, but nobody cares enough even to discipline
him.

It could be a husband or wife who is taken for granted
by the mate. This easily happens when we live together over
a period of time. How quickly we forget that the hunger of
love needs to be fed, just like physical hunger. Sometimes we
fence with one another to see who will bow to the other's
need first. Something of pride keeps us from saying what
the other is yearning to hear. Something of ego keeps us
from playing the servant role and forgetting about the recog-
nition. How desperately we need to stay close to the Lord
and walk in his steps. Today, is there some word that you
should say to someone, of love and appreciation? Pause in
quietness long enough to listen for the guidance that God
will give. Then *act* upon it. Then it is that you will hear
from Christ the "in as much" that says your feet are following his footsteps.

The real down-underneath foundation point of hunger
we will completely miss if we do not think of the Bread
which alone can satisfy for now and for eternity. In the sixth
chapter of the Gospel of John, beginning with verse 25, Jesus
defines this Bread, that he gives himself. He knew that the
crowd was following him because he had miraculously
fed the five thousand. When they follow him across the sea,
he tells them this. Then he says to them: "Do not labor for
the food which perishes, but for the food which endures to

eternal life, which the Son of man will give to you." They
asked, "What must we do, to be doing the work of God?"
Jesus answered, "This is the work of God, that you believe
in him whom he has sent." They remind him of the bread
that came to them in the wilderness and ask for a sign. He
responds with the classic passage: " . . . the bread of God is
that which comes down from heaven, and gives life to the
world . . . I am the bread of life; he who comes to me shall
not hunger, and he who believes in me shall never thirst."
Significant are the words that he said to the Samaritan woman: "Every one who drinks of this water will thirst again,
but whoever drinks of the water that I shall give him will
never thirst; the water that I shall give him will become in
him a spring of water welling up to eternal life."

The psalmist knew something of this source when he
declares: "For he satisfies him who is thirsty, and the hungry
he fills with good things" (Psalm 107:9).

The prophet Isaiah calls out the invitation: "Ho, every
one who thirsts, come to the waters; and he who has no
money, come, buy, and eat . . . !" In the glorious picture
of our eternal home which is to be found in the Book of
Revelation, we read: "They shall hunger no more, neither
thirst any more; . . . the Lamb . . . will guide them to the
springs of living water." The Bible is indeed rich with the
promise of the satisfying of this hunger and thirst in man-
kind.

The important thing, however, is, do you know this?
When the earthly trappings, as attractive as they are, cannot
assuage the longing in your soul, do you know the fulfillment that there is in *believing in Christ,* in resting yourself,
your life, and your loved ones in him? When you do know

it, the whole compulsion of your life will be to share it with others. Are you willing to be the vessel through which the Living Water can flow, and by which the Bread of Life may be shared? Begin where you are, in the lives of those closest to you. From there on Christ will lead the way.

Travel Guides

1. Make a real effort to inform yourself about the areas of need in your neighborhood, in your city, in your country, and around the world.

2. Find out what your church is doing in these areas.

3. Ask God for help to know where you can serve best.

4. Share with others the information you have gained and seek to enlist their help.

5. Do something special in the name of Christ today.

Prayer

The outstretched hands of the world, Lord, are all about me. Give me grace to begin where I am to be your distributor of the bread for the body as well as the soul. Make me a good steward of all that you have given me. In Jesus' name. Amen.

CHAPTER NINE

Into the Sickroom

In thinking of Christ's walk here on earth, certainly one of the things that immediately comes to mind is his ministry to the sick. Everywhere he went the sick were brought to him. In Matthew 8:14, we are told of the sickness of Peter's mother-in-law. And then we read: "He [Jesus] touched her hand, and the fever left her, and she rose and served him. That evening they brought to him many who were possessed with demons; and he cast out the spirits with a word, and healed all who were sick. This was to fulfill what was spoken by the prophet Isaiah, 'He took our infirmities and bore our diseases.'" In Matthew 14:14, we read of how he had compassion on them and healed their sick. The psalmist speaks of how he heals the brokenhearted and binds up their wounds (Psalm 147:3). Jesus makes clear that often a sickness is due to the imprisonment of sin, and when this can be confessed and forgiven, his touch brings wonderful healing.

Maybe it would be helpful, if we are really in earnest about walking where he walks, to consider how to visit the sick.

There are some people who, unless they permit God to change their frame of mind, should never enter a sickroom. They mostly make the patient worse. To visit an ill person and to just drip woe with every word and facial expression is to leave him feeling much worse than when you came. On the other hand, to enter gaily with an affectation of cheer, and pretend that nothing is wrong, is just as bad because it is false, and in playing out such a role, you impound your real self. There is nothing that conveys itself as readily as sincerity, in every area of life.

Listen to the word of a pastor's widow, which she wrote to the congregation and other friends, after her husband's victorious homegoing: "During the days of his illness, my husband and I both watched our reactions to people who thought they ought to be solicitous. By all means, I admonish you, Christians, never to put on a face of woe or commiseration. Be yourself, in your present joys, strengths, and problems. *Share your strength, not your pity!*" How then shall we make our approach to the sick?

Shall we first of all search our own hearts to see what our attitude is about sickness? No matter what disease might afflict you, would you be able to feel in your heart: "But it isn't too hard for God; with him, nothing is impossible!" With this would there be the calm certainty that, no matter what happened, he would be at your side to be your sufficiency? If this is the feeling you have for your own life, it will convey itself to others.

Before you make a sick call, stop and think: "If I were that person I am to visit, what kind of call would I want made on me?" Pause and pray that Christ will be in you as you make the visit; that his healing presence will flow through you. Then you will discover the joy of being his channel, of bringing healing love to the place where you go.

Unforgettable is the experience we had one Sunday evening. After a busy day we were weary, and anticipated the comfort and relaxation of the fireplace at home. As we were leaving church, my husband turned to me and said: "I can't get Lenore off my mind. I think we had better head toward George Washington Hospital to see her." "But," I protested, "you just saw her last night, and she was getting along nicely then. It's way past visiting hours." I knew my protests were foolish, though exceedingly human, and so we made our way to the hospital. Even though it was 10 P.M., my husband's clergyman's status admitted us, and we proceeded to the fifth floor, to the room of this friend.

I'll never forget her cry as we entered the room. "How did you know I have been praying you might come. How did you know how desperately I needed you!" Then she broke into convulsive sobs. After I got to her bedside and held her in my arms for a few minutes (praying silently in my heart) she calmed down enough to tell us her story. She had come to the hospital for a biopsy, for she had been having severe headaches for which the doctors could find no cause. Her mother had died of cancer, and lurking in this young mother's heart was this threat. She had two little children at home, and her imagination had simply gone wild, conjuring up all the fears the devil plants in our minds in times like these.

The real pay-off came that afternoon when a man whose wife was in the room across the hall came in to visit her. She told him that the doctors had assured her that her spinal test had indicated no malignant infection of any kind. To which this "well-meaning" friend had responded: "Oh, but don't believe them. Look at my wife. That is what they told her in Florida, and here she is. Don't believe them!" After he finally left, having planted this "encouraging" thought, Lenore was beside herself. Suppose they were hiding something from her; suppose they were afraid to tell her the truth; suppose . . . It must have been at this point that the Lord put it into my husband's heart to change our direction and head toward the hospital. Have you had the joy of knowing how God's Word can fill a need and change a climate? The pastor read: "Commit your way to the Lord; trust in him and he will act" (Psalm 37:5). Then the familiar 23rd Psalm from the heart, speaking the meaning of every sentence. You could just see that tense, taut body relax, and the change of the facial expression was a "before and after" experience.

When we finally came home, the telephone was ringing. Lenore's husband was on the line. "I don't know what you did to Lenore," he said, "but I want to thank you from the bottom of my heart. She just phoned me and said she knew she would have a wonderful night's sleep and thought maybe she would even be home for Christmas. Thanks a million!" Then we were able to tell him of the way that God worked in even changing our direction when we wanted to go home.

Lenore was home for Christmas, and you can imagine the happiness of that reunited family. Kleven, the three-year-old, was all smiles. When the neighbor came to visit she said to him, "Aren't you glad your daddy brought your mother home for Christmas?" Little Kleven's response was: "Not my daddy. It was God who did it." Kleven was right!

Not all hospital visits are as rewarding or as dramatic as this one. Sometimes I think that it is the test of the long haul that really tells the story. Visiting the chronically sick, the invalids, the aged—here is where the grace of Christ really shines. But what joy it is to plan little surprises, to even make laughter ring out through those rooms. We still chuckle when we think of Mary Hallin, 94 years old, and unable to take care of herself. As a ward of the community she was admitted to a hospital for chronic invalids and the senile. She had a delightful sense of humor. Being of Scandinavian extraction she liked some of the special delicacies associated with the Christmas festivities. So this one Christmas we filled a little jar of our home-prepared pickled herring *(sill)* and brought it to her with some "hardtack." She was delighted and put it away in the cupboard of her nightstand. The next time we came to visit her she laughed and said: "Pastor, I have never had my feet washed so often in all my life. When the nurse is out, I have my little feast of *sill,* and then quickly tuck it away before she comes back. The other day she came in and sniffed and said: 'Your feet smell. I think we had better wash them.' Believe me she gave them a scrubbing. Each time I have a little of the *sill* the same thing happens. I just let her go ahead and wash my feet. The *sill* tastes awfully good." You can imagine the gales of laughter that flowed from that sickroom.

How to visit the sick? I am reminded of a woman who went calling on a person that was ill, only out of a sense of duty. You understand, then, why the visit was a "dud" both for her and for the visited one. For when she was about to leave, the patient said to her: "Next time you come, won't you try to leave something of yourself here?" As Christians we should try to leave something of the fragrance of our Christ when we have made a call. If you pray about it before you go, he will enable you to do it. He will be right there with you!

There is another word of admonition. Don't wear the patient out, either by too much talking or too long a visit. Maybe the thing the sick one needs most at the time is a good listening ear. This is a real gift to bring to any conversation. Then watch your time so that you won't put the patient in the position of wishing you would go. A loving "look-in" can be a real tonic.

Every call may be different, and the procedure you follow in each may vary. Every personality, too, will have something unique to bring. Here again we must ask God for wisdom and guidance. Maybe you will not in every instance want to have devotions with the one you visit. Maybe you are timid about doing this at all. I have yet to find the person who wasn't grateful for a prayer. Below are listed some passages as samples of what could be shared with joy in the sickroom.

Psalm 91:1-12	Psalm 9
Isaiah 30:15	Philippians 4:4-7
John 15:7	Isaiah 26:3
Revelation 7:14-17	Deuteronomy 33:27
Psalm 103:1-5	Isaiah 40:28-31

Or a poem like this:

Morning Presence

O thou
who hast given me eyes
to see the light

that fills my room,
give me the inward vision
to behold thee in this place.

O thou
who hast made me to feel
the morning wind upon my limbs,
help me to feel thy presence
as I bow in worship
of thee.

CHANDRAN DEVANESEN
from *The Cross Is Lifted*

Or these two, written by lepers living on an island off the
coast of Japan:

In All Things, Victory

He hears me pray to him upon the deep,
When masts are gone and tattered sails are blown
By storms that drive my frail boat out to sea;
He hears, and sends the wind that wafts me home.

Naught that can come shall bring despair to me,
Gaining in all things more than victory!

He hears me pray to him when I am lost
Amid wild mountains, and no path can see;
He saves me from the beasts and from the night,
And gives the comfort of his strength to me.

He hears me pray to him when my tired feet
Struggle across the desert's burning sand;
With his own blood restores my fainting soul;
And to green pastures leads me by the hand.

The limits of the earth are wide and vast,
And vaster still its smiling dome of blue,
Yet through this space I always hear his voice,
"O little one," he says, "I died for you!"

My Lord in me has found a dwelling place,
And I in him. O glorious boon to gain
To be his temple! Gladly will I face,
In his great strength, all bitterness and pain!

NAGATA

A Song of Daily Life

Again, today, Lord,
Let me write
In characters of sweat and tears
Words that will bring
Thy children to the light.

And faith and hope and love
Will be
The warp and woof
Of fabric gay
That I would weave for thee
Today.

URAKO HAYASHI
Songs from the Land of Dawn

Poems such as these may be typed on a card, and after they have been read, left with the sick friend to be read again.

You don't share poetry with everyone. We ask God for grace to know the particular need of each patient and bring to that bedside the healing presence of the Christ in the way that will best speak to his needs.

Travel Guides

1. Make a list of people you know who are ill.

2. Pause and pray for each one.

3. Ask God to direct you to one or two to whom you can begin ministry.

4. Plan a time for the visit—and plan the visit.

5. Pave the way with prayer preparation.

6. After the visit be quiet before the Lord to inventory your experience.

Prayer

Lord, I want so much to be a channel of healing to others. Empty my heart of all pride and a mere sense of duty, if I am to so serve. Give me the winsomeness of your loving presence, and strengthen my faith so that it will bring its witness to the place to which you send me. Lord, I would follow you wherever there is need. Amen.

CHAPTER TEN

Into the Human Mind

The words mind, heart, imagination, are used inter-changeably in Scripture. At this point we see no purpose in going into a fine delineation of the difference in these words. Suffice it to say that we are such a composite, in the miraculous plan of God's creation, that the combination of the three makes up the real person which dwells in the shell of the body. There is no greater need today than to have Jesus walk deep into the country of this inner self. It will be necessary to do some dynamiting along the way, clearing out some underbrush and chasing away the reptiles that lurk in unsuspected places. It is a strenuous and costly journey. Are you willing to take it?

The crucial importance of the condition of this inner self is spoken to again and again in Scripture. Proverbs 23:7 reads (King James translation), "For as he thinketh in his heart so he is." Certainly there is no more forthright declaration of this than the words the Lord used as they are recorded in Matthew 15:19: "For out of the heart come evil thoughts, murder, adultery, fornication, theft, false witness, slander. These are what defile a man." In exposing the duplicity of the religious people of his day, as recorded in this same chapter, Christ uses no uncertain terms as he quotes from Isaiah: "This people honors me with their lips, but their heart is far from me." Earlier in his ministry he put the question to the crowd that was gathered about him (the preliminary comment of the Gospel writer is: "But Jesus, knowing their thoughts said . . . "), "Why do you think evil in your hearts?"

At this point we would do well to consider the seven things that the writer of the Book of Proverbs lists as things which the Lord hates: " . . . haughty eyes, a lying tongue, and hands that shed innocent blood, a heart that devises wicked plans, feet that make haste to run to evil, a false witness that breathes out lies, and a man who sows discord among brothers." The voice of the prophet Jeremiah cries out with its original concern today: "O Jerusalem, wash your heart from wickedness, that you may be saved. How long shall your evil thoughts lodge within you!"

Obviously, the seeds to our own destruction are within us, and the real world in which we live has little to do with the outward physical circumstances, but depends on *who* lives in our hearts and *who* directs the roadways of our minds. The poet Milton has put it succinctly: "The mind itself is its own place and can make a hell out of heaven and a heaven out of hell."

Perhaps we will be most helpful if we take a closer look at the seven things that are listed as "an abomination unto the Lord."

Haughty eyes. In these simple words may be found the key to the gate of our own destruction. When Christ walks into our minds, pride must go. In an age that preens itself on "self-made men," and "do-it-yourself," and "I am the master of my fate," this is the greatest roadblock. The pseudo-scientific intellectualism of our day scoffs at anything that it cannot master and preens the feathers of its vaunted importance. There is an increasing number of real intellectual scientific giants, however, whose very trademark is humility in the face of the amazing truths about the mobility of creation that they are just beginning to uncover. There are no "haughty eyes" in this group, but rather a deep sense of wanting to worship the Creator whose plan is greater than our finite minds can comprehend.

What in your life makes for "haughty eyes"? How many times have you declared yourself with the pontifical feeling that yours was the final word? What persons or classes of people have you looked down upon as being inferior and of less importance? When you look at someone whose outward appearance repels you, are you able to see beneath to the soul that Jesus Christ died to redeem? Do you easily shrug off people as being inconsequential? Perhaps the pertinent Scripture to true us at this point is that matchless section of Paul's Letter to the Philippians 2:4: "Have this mind among yourselves, which you have in Christ Jesus, who, though he was in the form of God, did not count equality with God a thing to be grasped, but emptied himself, taking the form of a servant, being born in the likeness of men." The writer goes on to say that Christ's humility had its final culmination in death, death on the cross. Are you willing to have Jesus dynamite away the roadblock of pride in your heart?

C. S. Lewis, in his book *Christian Behavior,* speaks of pride as being at the very center of Christian morals. He calls it the essential vice, the utmost evil. The sins of unchastity, greed, drunkenness are as flea-bites in comparison. His concluding statement is pretty inclusive: "Pride leads to every other vice; it is the complete anti-God state of mind." The amazing thing about this tool of the devil is the many-faceted appearance it has. It sits in the church and thinks: "Well, I'm not like Mrs. So-and-So." It breathes into the organized church with denominational dress and the thought: "We of my church have the simple, unvarnished truth of the Bible. And we have a special corner on it." Sometimes it is like the church-school teacher who taught the story of the publican and the Pharisee and ended with the prayer: "Thank you, God, that we are not like the Pharisee."

Of what are you most proud? Your position, your family, your appearance, the way you keep house, or the way you do your job in the office? Is it some work of your hands or your mind? Are you willing to put your entire self at the feet of Christ (including all the areas of pride you have now thought of) and acknowledge that without him you are nothing? The hymn writer has put it well:

> Forbid it, Lord, that I should boast,
> Save in the cross of Christ, my Lord;
> All the vain things that charmed me most,
> I sacrifice them to his blood.

A lying tongue. So crafty is the father of lies that he has people telling falsehoods of which they are hardly aware themselves. Perhaps the ace in his hand is that subtle deception that takes refuge in saying nothing. A failure to deny falsehood is as surely a lie as an untrue statement, yet often we cower before the courage that it takes to speak the truth and seek cover under this method. Something of the principle involved is illustrated by the story a friend tells of her father. Her mother, eager for a word of commendation about some piece of culinary art that she had placed before her husband, would eagerly ask: "How is it?" And his laconic reply would be: "Well, I ate it, didn't I?" What a word of praise!

Another method of the evil spirit that roams the earth is to involve us in half-truths and innuendoes. In no place is this more powerfully done than in the area of our religious beliefs. The graying up of our convictions until they are neither white nor black; the subtle, "Has God said . . . " or, *"If* you are the Son of God . . . " are methods the devil employed in the Garden of Eden and on the mount of temptation, and he is still using the same ones today.

Actually this perpetrator of untruth has a special method for each person and attacks him in his most vulnerable spot. What is yours? In what areas do you find it the hardest to stand for the truth? Could it be in connection with yourself, your relationships with others, your motives? If your reaction has been as you have been reading these lines: "Why, I pride myself on telling the truth. That's one thing I can say for myself," then I would say: "Beware!" Let the great Searcher of hearts flood your soul and X-ray every nook and cranny of your mind.

Hands that shed innocent blood. "But here," you say, "is an area in which I am not guilty! I have never shed innocent blood." Can you let yourself off that easily? As a part of a society that permits conditions to exist which are responsible for the shedding of innocent blood, do you not have guilt on your hands when you have shrugged your shoulders at a known condition and done nothing about it and cared less? If you were a mechanic in charge of conditioning an airplane and were careless about the check-up because you were involved in something else, and as a result of your carelessness that plane in flight crashed and all the innocent passengers aboard were killed, would you be guiltless? Yet in the communities in which we live there are housing conditions and legalized vices that are crippling the lives of innocent children, and most of us who bear the name Christian do nothing. There is this timely matter of race relations. How are you following Christ into this area? Would you rather shrug your shoulders and ask not to be involved? Are you willing to look beyond the color of any skin and see a brother, a sister, for whom Christ died?

Remember, too, Christ's interpretation of the Fifth Commandment: Thou shalt not kill. He said that if we have hate in our heart we have broken that commandment. Who can stand before the implication of this? With King David I would cry out:

Have mercy upon me, O God, according to thy steadfast love;
   according to thy abundant mercy blot out my transgressions.
Wash me thoroughly from my iniquity,
   and cleanse me from my sin.

A heart that devises wicked plans. It is interesting to note that the heart is spoken of in this listing of the seven in the center. Here is the seat of all that goes before and after. Here is the source of what our tongue says, of what our hands do, of what we think and are. Who rules your heart? Christ with his all-seeing eye would journey there and search out every labyrinthian passageway, every little bypath, every subtle detour, and clear the highway for his triumphal entry into your life. To make this reading more meaningful for your life, why don't you take a pencil right now and put down some of the blocked passages that are going to have to be cleared? What in your life does not square with his presence within you? The crux of the whole matter is to be found in honesty, honesty measured by his eternal standard who knows the desires and intent of our hearts.

Have you ever tried to make your way on a discarded road? A tree may have fallen across it, grass and debris may cover it, and travel is well-nigh impossible. The road in our heart must daily be cleared if the King of kings is to have it as his highway.

What about the debris that you find? What are you going to do with the rubbish? Give it to God, yes, but he has also pointed out a further step in the clearing process. Make restitution in the lives of people who have been affected by the clutter. This isn't easy; only the grace of God compels.

In our home not long ago sat a doctor and his wife who shared what an amazing transformation had taken place in their lives. These gifted folks were from Scotland and had spent fifteen years as medical missionaries in India. "But," said he, "I really wasn't honest with God in my work in India. I felt irritation and competition with a fellow doctor until I came to the point where I used dysentery as an excuse to get out of the field. It was only an excuse. I wasn't being honest. Not until I was quiet enough before God to have him face me with my real self and my true motives

did the change come." Then he quietly and humbly told
the thrilling story of being used in the years that followed
to heal the total man as he permitted Christ to work
through him. There was a terrific clearing of the highway
of his heart before it could become an open channel for
God. He related one instance of sickness after the other,
where as a man of God and as a doctor he was able to get
at the seat of the difficulty in the person's mind, and often
over night the asthma, or the headache, or the backache
cleared up. We felt as though we had been in the presence
of Dr. Luke.

The wife, too, told of facing this criterion of honesty and
having God's spotlight reveal areas of deception from her
past. Here she was, a grandmother, and yet she recalled
that when she was attending school in Scotland she had
"pinched" things; she recalled lies that she had told. At first
the thought of writing to the teacher to confess it after these
intervening years had horrified her. But she knew there was
no other solution. Once she set to writing the letters, it
came easily. And then she was *free*.

She also told that when she has a migraine headache or
some other such pain, she goes to the Lord and asks him
what it is in her mind and heart that is bringing this
about. She then waits in quietness before him. Invariably
he will show her some unkind motive or attitude she has
had, and when she has confessed it, and by God's grace
righted it, even to the point of going to the person and clearing the air, the pain leaves.

Lest you scoff too readily when you read this, friend, try
it. Put it to the test in the best laboratory available and
honestly use the prescription. It is the pattern that Scrip-

ture gives; it is the pattern the Lord used when he walked on this earth and healed people. In connection with a healing, how many times did he say: "Go and sin no more. Thy sins are forgiven thee"? Lest we be quick to judge others who may be suffering, a word of warning. There are cases of illness where pain is caused by organic pressures on the nerves or other internal conditions. You can't judge what may be happening to another person. You can suggest what has helped you. It is for you to try this heart-searching on yourself and then tell others the great and wonderful things the Lord has done for you.

Yes, the heart has an amazing way of devising wicked plans.

Feet that make haste to run to evil. When do your feet drag, and when do they go quickly? With joy do you run the errands of the Lord? Or with zest do you follow the way of the world? Take a look at your day and the attitudes you have toward the things that need to be done. Does God need to get into your feet? Another prophet spoke of another kind of feet: "How beautiful are the feet of those that preach good news." Which kind have you?

A false witness that breathes out lies. Go to the Epistle of James to learn in the simplest and plainest language about the devastation that the tongue causes. In our consideration of the lying tongue we have discussed some of the implications of this. Notice that ending the list of the things that the Lord hates, the false witness is linked with a man who sows discord among brothers. The former is the means of accomplishing the latter. What clever devices we use these days: innuendoes, ridicule, yes, even a deadly silence when the truth should be spoken.

What about the things you pass along? Are they the things that make for peace in your community, in the world? Have you ever stirred up animosity between others in order to raise your own stock? What a tool this is in the hands of the devil in the area of in-law relationships: a wife maligning her mother-in-law in order to build herself up in her husband's eyes; an employee spreading malicious accusations about a fellow employee in order to gain the favor of the boss. What nasty tricks our minds play with our tongues!

A man who sows seeds of discord among his brothers. As descriptive a Scripture passage as can be found for the man of our title is in 1 Timothy 6:4. "He is puffed up with conceit, he knows nothing; he has a morbid craving for controversy and for disputes with words, which produce envy, dissension, slander, base suspicions." There are people who seem to take a delight in controversy. Perhaps we would do better to say there are times in each of our lives when this spirit takes hold. Have you never passed along something about someone, which you afterwards wish you could recall because you see the harm that has been done? There are instances of whole communities being torn with strife because some had planted the seeds of discord or suspicion. There are families in constant turmoil because of this insidious practice. A mother may build up antagonisms in her children against their father, or vice versa. Envy and jealousy among brothers and sisters have been known to make a hell out of a home.

Sometimes the guise is pious. "I hate to tell you this, my dear, but I really think you ought to know . . . " and then follows the tripe that makes one want to vomit. Those aren't pretty words, but they are of the same flavor as the thing of which we speak. Have you been guilty of passing along something that caused trouble between people?

There is a word from Scripture on the positive side: "Then let us no more pass judgment on one another, but rather decide never to put a stumbling-block or hindrance in the way of a brother" (Romans 14:13). What a measuring stick for our sowing! We would spare ourselves some bitter regrets if we would pause and ask ourselves the question: "Will this create goodwill and peace? Will this heal rather than wound?"

There is one other pathway that I'd like to mention before we leave the traveling in the land of the mind. It is the mucky road of self-pity. If you want to get mired and worn out and discouraged, just travel this road. It really "does" you. I have listened to endless relating of the events of lives where the unexpressed but ever-recurrent theme and refrain is: "Poor me!" The amazing thing is that the people with this frame of mind have least to complain about actually, but they are the most to be pitied because they are slaves to themselves. Self-pity stinks, and it is an obnoxious road to travel. In the book *Cannibal Valley,* we are told of how the natives of a certain section of Dutch Guiana suddenly began wearing flowers in their noses. When the white men who had only recently come to this place inquired why they did this, the natives said that the white men had such a putrid smell that they wore the flowers to counteract it. No amount of perfume or flowers can cover the stench of one wallowing in the mud of self-pity. I can remember having to travel through a northern town where there was a wood pulp factory. If the wind blew in a certain direction, we would have to close all the windows of our car to try to keep out the heavily scented air. It almost asphyxiated us. Wood pulp smells are tame compared to that of self-pity.

When have you pitied yourself? About what? Ask God to show you.

Enough of detours and unnecessary ones at that! We need to recognize them in order to avoid them. If we follow closely upon the heels of the Lord, these are not the paths we will travel. The Apostle Paul has plainly given directions to the glory road in the mind when we follow the Christ. Philippians 4:8, in the New English Bible, reads: "And now, my friends, all that is true, all that is noble, all that is just and pure, all that is lovable and gracious, whatever is excellent and admirable—fill your thoughts with these things." Talk about mental health—here it is.

But, you say, how can I help what thoughts come into my mind? What produces thoughts? One very obvious thing that we need to be aware of is that the kind of reading we do directly affects our thinking. You can't steep yourself in literary muck that is so popular on today's market, and come out clean! The tragedy is that it is so difficult for us to remember good, and the evil sticks so insidiously. If you read the things that plant doubt and tear down faith, this is the kind of thinking that will hang like a cloud over your mind. If you read about faith and what it has done for others, and the miracle of God's grace in their lives, this becomes a strengthening to your own thinking along these lines. Every time that splendid little magazine *Faith at Work* comes, it is like a shot of spiritual penicillin against the nagging doubts so prevalent in today's world. In these pages is recorded the witness of one changed life after the other through the grace of a personal relationship with

Jesus Christ. I take new courage in our work, and instead of thinking: "That person is impossible; he will never change!" I am encouraged to think: "Christ is still walking among men and miraculously changing lives! He can do it here too; he has done it with me."

Of course, when we speak of our reading we would underscore and *capitalize* what it means to fill the mind with the truths of Scripture so that these become the very pattern of our thinking. How many times my sharp tongue has been stopped because from within has thundered the word: "And on her tongue was the law of kindness." And when there have been occasions for discouragement even in the kingdom work, what a reinforcement it is to hear the One who controls the universe say: "In the world is tribulation; but be of good cheer; I have overcome the world." Yes, there is a word to counteract every difficult mood, and for every confusing situation, if we will but search the Scriptures for it and then hide these words in our hearts that they may become a part of our unconscious thinking. *You think what you read!* What you feed the mind determines the kind of health it has!

I would like to challenge you to the discipline of great reading! Though there be much trash, thank God there is much that is stimulating, interesting, helpful—yes, and beautiful!

As previously mentioned, the main course of your diet should be the Bible. Do you know the joy of really studying it, searching it? There are fine helps available today. Dr. William Barclay of Scotland has done a whole series of studies on each book of the New Testament. These are in the form of daily Bible studies and are rich in background and insights and give much food for thought. You may not agree with all that the author says, but this is your challenge to make your own decision, according to your conscience and the light you have. Your own church publication house has fine things to suggest. For a study of the parables, try Dr. Helmut Thielicke's *The Waiting Father*. See if you will not find yourself in these matchless stories of Christ as you are aided by the contemporary presentation of Dr. Thielicke. A good number of his books have been translated into English. You may want to follow with: *How the World Began,* or *Our Heavenly Father* (a study of the Lord's Prayer), or *The Silence of God,* or *Man in God's World*.

One of the great Christian exponents of how the mind and spirit affect the body is the Swiss medic, Dr. Paul Tournier. *The Meaning of Persons, A Doctor's Casebook, Guilt and Grace, Escape from Loneliness, The Healing of Persons* —these are some of the choice offerings that have come from his facile pen. I invite you to sample this energizing fare!

We would recommend the works of Dr. Reuel Howe. In a little study group, try using *Herein Is Love,* or *The Creative Years,* or *Man's Need and God's Action*. Are you fed up on banal, superficial conversation? Probe *Dialogue* by the same author. Dr. Albert Day has a splendid volume, *Destiny and Dialogue,* on the same subject.

Consult your church publications for new reviews—and know the joy of expanded horizons. A delightful story is told about Bishop Quayle, who is sometimes called "The Skylark of Methodism." This was in the days when most traveling men rode the trains. The conductor became pretty familiar with these men and so as he punched the tickets he would inquire as to how business was in each line. When he came to the bishop, he took him for another salesman and so because he was new on that run, inquired, "And what do you sell, sir?" The bishop paused a moment and then looking up at the conductor, said: "Why sir, I sell horizons!"

There is an exercise that I must write about if you are truly interested in walking with Jesus into the land of the mind. This is the joy of memorizing—especially the Bible. A mood can be completely redeemed from ugliness if, through discipline, lines of Scripture can be called to mind.

A friend of mine was obsessed by fear to the point of a nervous breakdown. God put it into the heart of another friend to challenge her to memorize the 103rd Psalm. They were to do it together with even a bit of competition in it! That was the best medicine that sick, fear-ridden mind had received. Even the doctor marveled at what happened. Of course, coupled with this, was loving concern on the part of this same friend. The blessings of her Christian love flowed into the life of the distressed woman, and they knew real joy together as they memorized the matchless words of the psalmist!

> Bless the Lord, O my soul;
>   and all that is within me,
> bless his holy name!

What you see and surround yourselves with is also a factor in thought control. Let a young man fill his room with lurid pictures, and before too long his mind will be filled with lust and sex. Some people's eyes have become so "filmed over" by the movies they see that a rose or a sunset may go completely unnoticed, but the swing of a hip or the shape of a leg really catches the eye. What about the friends with whom you associate? Do they lift the level of conversation? Do you? Or do you each lower to the level of the least?

The Apostle Paul enjoins us to have in us the mind that is in Christ Jesus. If ever there was a realist, he was one. He could look right through the outward veneer of respectability among the professing religionists of his day and see the wormy thoughts and decaying hearts. But at the same time he could look into the eyes of a woman caught in adultery and see a woman to be redeemed, a potential daughter of the King. His love covered all the ugliness he had to look through to see this inner potential. Roland Hayes, asked for the secret of his wonderful stage presence, said, "I always sing to the king in the audience." Do you see in every person you meet a soul to be redeemed?

There is another point on the matter of what makes our thoughts. In the kind of world in which we live we cannot isolate the evil, so we rub elbows with it. An evil thought may come into your mind, but you can prevent it from nesting there and raising a brood of offspring. The power of Jesus' name to do this is miraculous, because his name reverently spoken sets to route all that is evil. Breathe a prayer, and substitute a thought of beauty or purity or love. Notice that in this Philippian quotation, the apostle uses the expression: " . . . all that is lovable and gracious . . . . " What a beauty treatment this is for any face! If you are thinking lovable and gracious thoughts, their imprint will be on your visage, your tongue, and your whole being. Can you imagine a person thinking such thoughts and slouching? The whole body is toned up when we think Christ's thoughts after him.

Satan is abroad in the world today seeking to captivate men's minds. He uses such gimmicks as: "If there is a God . . . " and "You yourself are the King of Creation . . . " and "The world is a hopeless mess . . . " and "What can little you do?" and so on *ad infinitum*. But there is *another* striding across the turbulent waters of this earth. Sometimes in the quietness of a morning he speaks; sometimes it is when you stoop to help a little child, or pause to succor a needy one; or it could be while you are busy about your home, or engrossed in your office; you might be walking down a crowded pavement, or all alone on a schmahl-swept desert; maybe you are in a hospital room or bending over the casket of a loved one. Wherever—listen. He is speaking to you personally, and only if you shut your ears you will not hear! He is saying:

"As your day, so shall your strength be . . . "

or

"Inasmuch as you have done it unto the least of these my brothers, you have done it unto me . . . "

or

"Martha, you are anxious about many things. Simplify your life . . . one thing is enough . . . "

or

" . . . lo, I am with you always . . . "

or

"Do you want to be made well? All things are possible to him who believes . . . "

or

"Let not your heart be troubled . . . you believe in God; believe also in me. In my Father's house are many mansions . . . "

or

"In the world there is tribulation. But be of good cheer. I have overcome the world!"

Listen, my friend, and believe, and follow!

Travel Guides

1. Try to recall what thoughts have passed through your mind today. Have they been the kind that would pass the censorship of Christ?

2. Begin memorizing sections of Scripture. How about starting with the 103rd Psalm or the 34th?

3. In what areas do you feel sorry for yourself? Let Christ take them over.

4. Every morning take some thought from Scripture and call it to mind often throughout the day.

Prayer

Lord God, cleanse my mind of all that clogs its channels. I want your Holy Spirit to guide my thinking! Give me healthy, hopeful, happy thoughts to bless the lives of others. In Jesus' name. Amen.

CHAPTER ELEVEN

Into the Lives of Prisoners

Yes, if you are to walk where Jesus walks, you'll even go to prison!

The "prison" chapters of the Bible make dramatic reading. Beginning at Genesis 41:14, you have the amazing account of Joseph and his release. Acts 5:19 contains another jail delivery. We read: "But at night an angel of the Lord opened the prison doors and brought them [the apostles] out." Acts 12 has still another thrilling account with its climax in verse 7: "And behold, an angel of the Lord appeared [to Peter], and a light shone in the cell; and he struck Peter on the side and woke him, saying, 'Get up quickly.' And the chains fell off his hands." Acts 16 unfolds God's wonderful interventions in the release of prisoners. This time it was Paul and Silas who had been imprisoned. They were singing praises to God when "suddenly there was a great earthquake, so that the foundations of the prison were shaken; and immediately all the doors were opened and every one's fetters were unfastened" (v. 26). The prophet Isaiah foretold something of this redemptive work of Christ when he says: " . . . To open the eyes that are blind, to bring out the prisoners from the dungeon, from the prison those who sit in darkness . . . " (Isa. 42:7). Yes, the memorable words of Christ in the great kingdom chapter of Matthew are: "I was in prison and you came to me." But you say, "What business have I in prison?" Immediately we would reply: "The Lord's business!"

Is it the way of Christ to wipe his hands of those who have fallen? Thank God, no, for where would I or any of us be if this were so? If we believe there is forgiveness and a chance to begin again in his grace for each one of us, should we not believe this for those who have transgressed civil law so that they are imprisoned for their transgressions? What are we doing to put their feet in the right path? The incidents of repetition in the case of offenders is often a sad commentary, not so much on their weakness as on our indifference to their plight. What chance does a fellow with a prison record have to get a job when he comes out? Who will help him to a new beginning?

Do you want an exciting dimension to your Christian life? Investigate in your community as to what opportunities there are for you to venture into this kind of service. Maybe you would begin by visiting the prison and helping with handicraft classes; maybe the prison chaplain could recommend someone to you for whom you could provide a home while that person is looking for a job, and getting off to a new start. As a Christian, it should be your responsibility to find out what is happening in your penal institutions in the line of rehabilitation opportunities.

Another great area of need is for Christian love and concern for the mentally imprisoned. Doctors tell us now that many people in mental institutions could be released and would get well if there were someone to love them. You begin with as simple a program (in cooperation with the hospital, of course) as visiting such a place and playing games with the patients or maybe just letting them talk to you. What a joy to see an imprisoned mind emerge through the X-ray treatment of concern and love! Some of our most priceless experiences were at St. Elizabeth's in Washington, D.C. I am sure that the prayers and blessing of Agnes Frodeen still bear fruit in our lives, even though she has long since gone home to be with her Father. Here was a woman who some thirty years ago had a breakdown, and because the only thing they knew to do with such people who had no means was to incarcerate them, she had spent all these years in this mental institution. By the time we came to know her, the mental hospital was her sanctuary, and we were unable to woo her out of it. This did not prevent us from bringing our love into it. For us, she was our prayer partner, and followed every facet of our work by claiming God's promises for us.

There was a young man whom the doctor would not release unless there would be a home for him, at least for the first three months after his hospitalization. It was something to see the opening up of that bound personality through the ongoing weeks. What a joy it was when he could take a job. Now he is married and has a family and is a wonderfully concerned Christian citizen in his town. There is no more rewarding experience than to be used by the Lord in this loving work of offering release to the captives. Someone so aptly expressed what can happen: "I love you because you are helping to make out of the lumber of my life not a tavern but a temple."

The chaplain of the District of Columbia's Women's Reformatory came to me one night after I had conducted the weekly Bible class out there and said: "You had better talk to Peg. She doesn't want to live any more. She thinks there is no hope for her." Peg was in her late fifties, and had been in and out of that institution 100 times for alcoholism and its concomitant effects. I'll never forget the dejected picture she made as she huddled on the stool in the corner of her room. "There's no use, Mrs. Nelson. I'm no good. God has given me a chance again and again, and look where I am! You had better just give me up." After a little while of our sharing, she began to yield and said: "But where will I go when I come out? Everyone is fed up with me. I have no money and no place to go." Without stopping to consider all that might be involved (or was it the Holy Spirit?) I said: "Oh, you can come to our home. I'm sure God wants something better for you, and maybe he can use us to help."

On my 25-mile ride back into Washington that night I thought, "What have I done? I haven't consulted my husband about this. Our youngest daughter was still at home. Was this fair to her?" Then I remembered what had happened in our home the other day. Without warning, my husband appeared at the noon hour with a man obviously in need of help. He not only needed clothes, he also needed food and an opportunity to wash. While this new-found "friend" was in the bathroom, my husband came out and said: "Well, he came to church, and after I had heard his story I took him into the chapel and knelt in prayer with him. While I was on my knees, God said to me in the words of James: 'What does it profit, my brethren, if a man says he has faith but has not works? Can his faith save him?

. . . what use is it for a man to have faith when he does nothing to show it? If a brother or sister is ill-clad and in lack of daily food, and one of you says to them, "Go in peace, be warmed and filled," without giving them the things needed for the body, what does it profit? So faith by itself, if it has no works, is dead.' So here he is, and we'll have to keep him over the weekend, so I can help him get started on Monday morning."

The upshot of this adventure wasn't without its edge of humor either. My husband thought that his clothes most likely would fit the man, so he went into his wardrobe to find a pair of trousers. The only one that fit was his very best pair, which he had hardly worn himself! So the next morning this needy friend accompanied us to church in my husband's gladdest "rags." The postscript to this little interstice is the best of all: Two months later, having been able to see this man get on his feet and get back to his home, we received a heart-warming letter from his mother. It was golden pay.

All of this passed through my mind as I rather automatically guided the car along Shirley Highway. With the anticipation of an understanding heart to greet my commitment, I burst into the living room and explained to my partner this new challenge. How thankful to God I was when he said: "Of course we must do it. There is only one thing I ask, and that is that the reformatory doctor gives Peg an examination so that we don't unduly subject Mary to unwanted disease."

So Peg came to live with us, and the whole of the story will have to be told another time. Suffice it to say that over a period of seven years, years of victory and defeat, but years of God's constant forgiving grace, she was in and out of our home, until that last time when she was sick and the doctor said there was a very bad heart condition. I'll never forget that Wednesday night. I had been out for the Bible class again, and when I came home, Peg was sitting in front of the fireplace with my husband. In the face of her desperate physical condition, she had sought solace again in the oblivion of the bottle, and had presence of mind enough to call him. He found her in one of the usual haunts, before she had completely drowned herself. He had brought her home again and now they were talking over a cup of coffee. Another friend (with the same problem) was with her, and so I prepared the twin beds in Mary's room for these guests. (Mary was now away at college.) Then I joined the group about the fireplace. Peg was talking: "I know one thing; no matter how much I have sinned, Christ forgives me, and I am in the hollow of his hand, and no one can take me from there." After a bit we suggested it might be good for all of us to get some rest, and so we retired.

The next morning I thought I would let the women sleep as long as possible, so I made no effort to arouse them until after my morning chores were done. I knocked on their bedroom door with a breakfast tray in my hand. It was Clara's voice that responded: "Come in." As I entered she whispered: "Peg has been resting so quietly that I didn't want to disturb her." But it didn't take more than one look at Peg's face (it was turned to the wall so that Clara had not been able to see it) for me to know that she was really resting; her boat had pulled in on the shore of eternity. There was a momentary shock, and then joy as I remembered her witness of the night before.

We had to go through her effects for anything to pass on to her family. There was one thing I kept; tucked into her billfold was a typewritten card, dated the week after she had come to our house that first time. It is my treasured possession now. It reads: "Dear God, thank you for sending a Good Samaritan into my life to help me when I thought all hope was gone. Thank you for showing me that your love never gives up. Thank you, Christ, for being my Savior. Bless this home and everyone in it. And continue to let your love shine through it. Amen."

"I was in prison, and you visited me."

There are many kinds of prisons. Sometimes I wonder how many "free" people there really are. I wonder how often we do not imprison ourselves! We look out through bars of fear, and hatred, and resentment, and jealousy, and wonder that our spirits do not have wings and who can stand up and say that he does not constantly fight the isolating wall of self?

There is a Friend who wants to visit you in whatever prison you may be, and there is no prison in all the world from which he cannot free you if you will but put your trust in him. He may come in the quiet of the night and gently knock at your door. He may come in the midst of a turbulent struggle and speak with his still small voice. Listen to him—and open. *He has the power to set you free!*

Travel Guides

1. How concerned are you about the people who come into court and are behind bars?

2. What do you know about the penal institutions of your community and the spiritual ministry of them?

3. Is your church doing anything to bring Christ's redemption to these people?

4. Think of your friends. Are there those who are spiritually imprisoned to whom you could minister?

5. Examine your own life. Are you free, in Christ?

Prayer

Thank you, Lord, for what your dying on the cross and rising again did to break the power of sin forever. Forgive me when sometimes I live as if this had never happened. O God, thank you for the freedom of faith. In the loving compulsion of what this means to me, send me into the lives of others with the message: "You can begin again! Christ has set you free!" Amen.

CHAPTER TWELVE

Into Our Home

It is interesting to recall the backdrop of the homes Jesus visited when he walked this earth The Oriental idea of a family is that it is a little kingdom within itself where the father is the supreme ruler. This pattern also pertains in the Middle East. In the Hebrew tradition the mother was a real factor in the training of the children. Proverbs 31:1 speaks of "The words of Lemuel, king of Massa, which his mother taught him." In writing to Timothy, the Apostle Paul speaks of how as a child Timothy had learned the Scriptures and then later refers to the faith of Timothy's mother and grandmother as a point of influence in the young man's life.

As the boys grew older they went to rabbinical schools where the Scriptures were their textbooks. But at this point the Bible speaks about the father instructing the sons. "Hear, my son, your father's instruction" (Prov. 1:8). A unity of purpose in regard to the religious life was certainly one of the main factors in the stability and integrity of the home.

The home of Lazarus and Mary and Martha was a favorite resting place for Jesus. For us it was a real thrill to pause at the little village of Bethany outside of Jerusalem and imagine the scenes so graphically described in Scripture. I presume the hospitality we have known from some of our Arabian friends would be similar to the practices of the Bethany home, except for one basic difference. Here the men are entirely separated from the women, whereas Jesus sat and visited with Mary and Martha. In a home of the old pattern in Arabia there are cushions around the wall for your sitting comfort. In the dwellings of the wealthy there are luxurious Oriental rugs. The people are exceedingly hospitable and ply you with food. They may first offer you their coffee in tiny handleless cups. This liquid is very sweet and thick and flavored with cardamom. It is good the cups are small, yet that ever-present beak-nosed coffee pot is right there to fill them.

The main dish for a meal is rice which may be garnished with raisins and nuts. These folks are skilled in making rice flavorful and good. Of course, there is lamb and most likely chicken. For the most part, you don't use utensils but break off the section of the animal or the bird that you want with your hand.

My husband was privileged to be invited to a feast given in our neighboring village for the king. There were eighty sheep on huge brass trays. These thoroughly roasted animals were placed atop mountains of rice. On smaller trays there were dozens of chickens. The procedure was to break off the limb or pull out the hunk of meat that was your choice.

Just what the Lord was fed in the Bethany home we don't know. We do know that he loved to stop there. Someone has said, "The greatest gift that any human being can give to another is the gift of understanding and of peace."

This quality must have been the one that drew Christ again and again to the home of Lazarus, Martha, and Mary.

Would this characterize your home? Understanding and peace! What a rare gift for a woman to bring to her husband and children! What a quality for a man to have in his home! How is such an ideal attained?

The answer is so simple that people won't believe it. Maybe the rub is that, simple though it is, it has a real price. It is to get ourselves out of the way so that Jesus Christ may dominate our homes. When this happens, there is peace and understanding and joy.

In our parsonage set-up through the years we have been called upon to counsel in several different home situations, some of which were on the verge of dissolution because of tensions and lying and false standards and lack of discipline. In each instance the beginning of the solution was that one member of the family would so live the love of Christ as to begin to change the atmosphere. Let's take a look at the situations.

Here is an instance of a mother who had had a partial breakdown. She had been lax in the disciplining of her children, which had been a source of irritation to her husband. In her state of nervous collapse it seemed that her whole house was falling down on top of her. So she ran away from the situation as much as possible, with the result that the children became worse in their lack of regard for authority. In counseling with the teenage daughter and asking her cooperation on behalf of her mother's health, we found that she was full of resentment and rejection. Only self-pity dominated her immediate response. But we prayed that she might be the key and encouraged the younger sisters and brothers to help her. At first the response seemed nil; then there came real answer to prayer. She rose to the fact that she had been appealed to; she began to pray earnestly for help; she forgot her own selfish rebellion in the desire to help her mother. She became the key to a new atmosphere in that home, as she learned to bring her frustrations to God in prayer and to seek his aid for all the things that bothered her. The family began to pray together and to worship together. The mother's breakdown was averted and a family was restored.

Then there was the situation that my husband had written off as one almost impossible to resolve. We were introduced to it in a very dramatic way. We were out calling one night in Washington, and our teenage daughter was home alone. The door bell rang (it was about 10 p.m.) and answering it, she found an inebriate man, clutching a knife and saying: "Is my wife here? Are you hiding my wife?" Mary responded that she wasn't here (the wife had stayed with us one night when she had fled from this man, but now had found more permanent lodging). "Well then," he said, "I am going out to kill myself!" "Oh, don't, please don't," was Mary's response. "Please come in and wait. I'm sure my dad can help you!" and with that she opened the door for him to enter. (Many times we have felt that the guardian angels were working overtime.) She bade him be seated in the living-room while she quickly made a cup of coffee. This she knew she should do, for many another alcoholic had sought refuge at this same door. But the minutes dragged on, and we did not return. The constant reiteration was that there was no use in living if his wife wouldn't come back. "But God will help you," Mary responded. He had arisen from the chair and was about to go out into the night, when we drove up.

For months the pastor worked with both husband and wife, trying to find grounds for reconciliation. One day we would think there was hope, and the next day things looked impossible again. They were very much in our prayers, and we pleaded with them to turn to God in prayer. We went on our vacation, and when we came back we learned they had left the city to return to their home town. How thrilled we were a year later at Christmas to receive a Christmas card with the picture of a lovely baby, and on the back side a note which told how their home had been reunited; how God was blessing them, and that they had found warm and vital fellowship in a church; and a final beautiful word of gratitude for the patience and love that had directed them to their source of help. Well, that was about the best Christmas present we had that year. As we read this message, our comment was: "Nothing is too hard for God!"

One could go on and on with the evidence of Christ's transforming power in the home. Space does not permit it. For most of us the situations are not as dramatic as these mentioned. The irritations are daily drippings, and submerged resentments because we feel the other parties live lives of quiet desperation, barely enduring, when they might be living lives centered in Christ where they have wings.

Where do we begin? With ourselves. Here is the rub. Scripture speaks of each counting the other more worthy and being willing to be servant. You ask for grace to have this attitude, and let God take care of the others. You will find that as you go to him in prayer, he will enable you and put upon your heart ways of bringing healing to the situation. From this you will receive such deep quiet joy that you will be willing to even be a door mat and find real victory in his grace conquering your own self-righteous spirit.

When Jesus Christ comes into a home, even in through the avenue of only one person to begin with, the atmosphere changes. One of our friends said that when she and her husband had come to a new relationship in Christ they went to visit their daughter on their vacation. After the first couple of days, the daughter said to her mother: "What has happened to you and Dad? You are like two newlyweds! You used to get into each other's hair. What is it that has made the change?" And the mother's reply was: "It isn't 'it.' We have rededicated ourselves to Christ, and he has made the difference. We've discovered that instead of arguing about our differences, if we pray about them, God gives us understanding, and we come to a happy agreement. It's wonderful!"

My real laboratory is my own heart. Let me tell you about how God really worked on me one night. We had been keeping a pretty rugged pace as my husband was having to fill a vacancy in the neighboring oil village in the interim between pastors. After we had traveled the fifty miles across the hot desert to this town, the hours had sped by with the responsibility of a service, a Bible class, a children's group, and then a young people's group in the early evening. We had made the return fifty miles through the early evening hours and arrived home about nine o'clock. As we were turning down our street, I noticed a couple of friends heading for the movie, and the thought occurred to me: "Wouldn't it be good to relax at the cinema." I mentioned it to my better half, saying, "I wonder what is on at the movies tonight!" He was tired, and his response was: "Well, you know how to find out. Ask the recreation office." Well, this started my dander, because I quickly thought, "Now, as the man in the family, if he cared enough, couldn't he do that?" But I didn't give up that easily. I stubbornly went to the phone to make the inquiry, all the time feeling like a very abused person. The title that the man at the other end of the line mumbled didn't sound as if I would be glad I had insisted that we go; and anyhow, what do you think? My better half had relieved himself of his clothing and, in his pajamas and dressing gown, was locating the most comfortable chair, and was quickly ensconced in *The Christian Century*.

This crowning touch of cooperation almost undid me. Hadn't I tried to be helpful through the day? Weren't we in this thing together? Hadn't my whole life changed in the pattern necessitated by this isolated place? Why, the grievances piled up so thick and fast within me that my colon was about to have convulsions. I'd go back into the bedroom and put on the best pout I was capable of.

Then God gently knocked. He reminded me what I had been teaching the women in the Bible class that day. He reminded me that instead of thinking of what I wanted, why spoil this evening? Here was our comfortable home and a million things to be thankful for.

I didn't capitulate immediately. I'm too stubborn a gal for that. But God didn't give up. He put it into my mind to answer two letters from elderly friends which had blessed my life that past week. (How little I knew that while I was writing the one letter, God was calling the name of one of those friends.) By the time I had finished one note, the poison was seeping out. When I completed the second letter, I went into the living room and said: "How about a game of Scrabble?" You see, this is what he had wanted to do, because he finds it such good relaxation. We played our game, and I went to bed. (I wonder if there wasn't some self-righteousness in me yet! But God never gives up.) The next morning I awakened early, and began reviewing the preceding evening. I was ashamed of my childishness, and when my husband opened his eyes, I said: "Forgive me for being foolish last night. I should have thought of what you needed!" And so we had a great day.

Noah Webster was asked how he came to write the dictionary. His response was that he had a word with his wife, and one word led to another. Sometimes the silences are more deadly than the words. Someone needs to yield! "The greatest gift that any human being can give to another is the gift of understanding and of peace." How often we ruin the atmosphere because we think of what the other person should do for us!

Nothing is too hard for God *if you will let him begin with you.* There is no situation in any home that he cannot change.

When Jesus comes into a home, the family is going to want to worship together, in the home and in the church. Some of our most happy remembrances are the worship periods about the table. Here we were drawn together in the presence of the unseen Guest; here we knew the joy of prayer power as we recounted all the wonderful answers that were obvious. Laughter abounded and teasing, because before God there is no status, and we were all together as his children. Oh, that every home might know the ineffable joy of such hours, the armoring for difficult times ahead. Someone has to take the initiative and begin. Do you have a family altar? Is it alive with the presence of God? Why don't you ask him for grace to be used in this respect?

I wish families would memorize hymns and passages from Scripture together. It can be fun this way. What a blessing these things hid in the heart become in times of stress. It is easiest when the children are little. Young Mother or Father, give yourself to this opportunity when you have your children about you. They will bless you for it in the days to come. When Jesus Christ lives in a home, it becomes a foretaste of the home which awaits those who love him.

The fruits of his presence are felt in every area: in the handling of finances, in attitudes toward work and study, in sharing responsibility for the tasks to be done about the home, in the attitude toward neighbors and all our fellow men; in participation in the work of his church; in the stewardship of all of life. He wants to bless every household. Why won't we let him?

Travel Guides

1. Write down the things about your home which you would like to be different.

2. Are these the things God would want to be different?

3. How can you be used to be a part of the answer?

4. At the table, share some way God has answered prayer. Encourage the children to participate in sharing these things as well as in the other things that happen to them.

5. Set some small beginning of a pattern memorizing sections of Scripture. Make it fun as you do it together.

Prayer

Lord, the devil is trying so hard to break up our homes. He tries to get into everyone. Fill us so with your presence that he will find no room. Amen.

CHAPTER THIRTEEN

To Our Eternal Home

In Vilhelm Moberg's book *A Time on Earth* there is related the tragic story of a man who felt that his time on earth was wasted. There is a truth that threads through each chapter: You have this one life, this time on earth. In one memorable instance, an older brother says to a younger one: "Always think to yourself, I'm here on earth just this once! I can never come back again! Take care of your life! Take good care! Don't waste it. For this, now, is your time on earth."

Scripture is full of the exhortation for us to be aware of the opportunity of *now*. "Choose you this day whom you will serve"; ". . . redeeming the time for the days are evil . . ."; " . . . now is the day of salvation"; " . . . work for the night is coming" are a few of many instances pointing up the quick passage of time. But thank God, Scripture also flings wide the gate at the end of the road, to assure us that in Christ there is something beyond. He thunders across the ages: "Because I live, you, too, shall live."

Perhaps no one thing in the Dhahran community caused more people to stop and think about the fragile thread on which this life hangs than the disaster of MEA 444. This is the jet flight from Beirut to Dhahran that comes in about midnight a couple of times a week. This being a Moslem country, the weekend is Thursday and Friday, and so the Friday night flight is very popular. I doubt that there is anyone in camp who has not flown in on the 444. On this particular Friday a schmahl was playing around these parts. Now a schmahl (for those of you not too familiar with the vagaries of the desert) is a sand storm in pretty much the proportions of a blizzard, only the element that is hurled around is sand instead of snow. One plane came in (although the pilot was drenched from the perspiration caused by his nervousness) and another overflew. The third pilot with its 49 passengers crashed into the sea of Half Moon Bay.

Because of the poor visibility there were hours when no one knew the whereabouts of the plane. There were hopes of its having landed somewhere on the desert, so crews were sent out in all directions. It wasn't until Saturday morning that all land crews were called off, for the tip of the wing had now been sighted in the sea. My husband was called with the other two clergymen to be at the shore scene of operations, and so I accompanied him. The hope was always that someone might be floating; someone might be alive. I shall never forget the launching of "rescue operations." Every available skill had been called into action, and every man was giving his very best. Nor was it until all the bodies had been recovered but one (and this after several days of unwearying search) that the operations were called off. Some were still strapped to their belts and held fast with the wreckage at the bottom of the sea. Some were found floating on the opposite shores, having been jerked loose from the plane by the impact of the water. Those were traumatic days as the search went on.

The passenger list? Well, each person on that plane is a story by itself. Here was a young mother who had been on a holiday to Beirut. She had been tired and weary from the cares of her three children and the isolation of this desert living, so her husband had sent her to Beirut for rest and relaxation. There was a daughter coming home for a visit with her parents to share with them a newly announced engagement. There were executives returning from business trips. There was the T.W.A. manager returning to his family. There was the Allen family: Tom and Imogene (the Dad and Mom) and their two little blonde girls, Terry and Jean.

I shall never forget our last remembrance of this wonderful Christian family. I had been ill, and on the Sunday previous to their vacation, they had come to our house for a get-well visit. Imogene had made a lamb cake, and the two girls so proudly bore it in on its silver tray to our house. There was an Easter glow in the joy of sharing. This family had gone on short leave to fulfill one of the deep desires of their lives: to visit the place where Jesus walked. Their original ticket called for them to return on Sunday night, but because they had been able to expedite their Jerusalem visit, they were returning two days earlier. Tom was one of the finest teachers we had in our Dhahran school.

There were two other teachers aboard that fatal plane. One had gone to Rome to meet his fiancee and there they were married and were returning from their honeymoon. The other was the art teacher who had given herself so liberally through the six years she had been teaching in Dhahran. Well, as you can see, everyone in the community was touched in one way or another.

Isn't it strange that often it takes the tragedies of life to draw us together? The joint memorial service held in the school the following Monday is one no one who attended can forget. The Roman priest and the Episcopalian and other Protestant ministers conducted the service, and their joint choirs sang. The resurrection words of the victorious Christ brought their powerful witness from the lips of each of them. The closing hymn sung by the united choirs was "A mighty fortress is our God." In this hour of tragedy we had joined hands as we sought the comfort that only God could give. There was triumph in the lives of those who knew the reality of the words of our Christ: "I am the resurrection and the life. He that believes on me, though he die, yet will he live."

A half hour after our return from the service, my husband received a telephone call from one of the company officials. The man said: "A miracle happened at that service. Before, this camp was filled with fear and tension and uncertainty. The seeds of faith planted at that service have made all the difference in the world. How grateful I am."

The crash of the 444 was not the only disaster that week end. It seemed as if everything compounded. Our Protestant Fellowship has yearly what we call Oasis Day. This is a time when missionaries are brought in to share inspiration and insights. We had been thrilled at the prospect of a visit from Bishop Chandu Ray, whom we had met at a retreat at Green Lake, Wisconsin. Born a Brahmin of a gifted, well-endowed family, this humble, great Christian man had a story to tell that we were eager to share with our parishioners. He was due to arrive at 1 A.M. Thursday. My husband had picked up a virus that day that caused a rising temperature, so I insisted that he go to bed.

Accordingly, I joined the president of the council in meeting the Bishop. Some untoward circumstances at the airport delayed our getting him released for two hours, and it was crowding four o'clock when I finally fell into bed. Sleep had done the run-away by this time, for the circumstances of the Bishop's delay were a real cause of concern, so we lay in bed discussing them. It was about five-thirty when I finally fell into deep sleep, only to be rudely awakened at 6:30 by the ringing of the telephone. A nurse from the hospital was informing us that one of our fine Indian women who had been "care-taking" some American children while their parents were in the States, had been stabbed by a prowler, and that she was bleeding to death. Immediately my husband arose and went to the hospital to be with the distraught husband and to be in prayer for Surim's healing. He spent the entire morning there, as again and again they fed blood into this frail little woman, hoping to get the pressure up enough to operate. Her liver had been slashed.

Finally, the doctors decided to go in regardless, as their only hope, and so set about the operation of sewing up the liver. Her miraculous recovery, as well as the story of the shock to the community that such a thing could happen within our seemingly protected walls, is a story by itself. Suffice it to say that her gallant fight and sturdy faith, coupled with the skills God gave the physicians and nurses, all of them impowered by a great force of prayer, resulted in the recovery of this little lady. And after only two weeks on her feet she was able to make the trip to her beloved India and be reunited with her children.

But you can see what I mean about that week end, for the next night was the 444 crash. What does all of this have to do with Jesus' walk into our eternal home? It was like a dynamite blast from our affluent lives to the realization of how utterly passing is our time on earth.

The Bible had come alive in many hearts in a new and vivid way. "So teach us to number our days that we may get a heart of wisdom" (Psalm 90:12). "Look carefully then how you walk, not as unwise men but as wise, making the most of the time, because the days are evil" (Eph. 5:15). "I mean, brethren, the appointed time has grown very short" (1 Cor. 7:29). "Conduct yourselves wisely toward outsiders, making the most of the time" (Col. 4:5).

So many of the words of Job come to mind: "My days are swifter than a weaver's shuttle." "Now my days are swifter than a runner." Or again the words of the psalmist: "Behold, thou hast made my days a few handbreadths, and my lifetime is as nothing in thy sight" (Psalm 39:5). Again in Isaiah we find such descriptive figures as: "My dwelling is plucked up and removed from me like a shepherd's tent" (38:12). And in the Book of James, in answer to the question: "What is life?" we have the answer: "You are a mist that appears for a little time and then vanishes," so, the writer warns, you ought to say, "If the Lord wills, we shall live and do this and that." We are reminded of this constantly by our Moslem friends who accompany everything they say by the phrase: "Inshalla!" which being interpreted means, "As Allah wills."

More than this finger of warning, though, were the

glorious affirmations of our faith in Jesus Christ who conquered death. With what a ringing assurance into this situation came the words: "I am the resurrection and the life" (John 11:35). What power of victory in the challenge: "O death, where is thy victory? O death, where is thy sting?" (1 Cor. 15:55), or "What is it that overcomes the world but he who believes that Jesus is the Son of God?" (1 John 5:5). Like the Balm of Gilead were the words of Christ to those who would put their trust in him: "Let not your hearts be troubled; believe in God, believe also in me. In my Father's house are many rooms; if it were not so, would I have told you that I go to prepare a place for you? And when I go and prepare a place for you, I will come again and I will take you to myself, that where I am you may be also" (John 14:1-3). So, in our Bible classes, in our conversations, we have been talking about how ephemeral this life is, and all the things we so desperately strive for, and how glorious are the promises of eternity with Christ. What does it mean to walk "home" with him?

We were overwhelmed by the need of folks thinking this through the days following the disaster. Women, filled with fear, couldn't face the prospect of boarding a plane for long leave. The incidents of nervous collapse were multiplied. Counseling became nearly a full-time job. One mother so identified herself with one of the mothers on the plane as to be dead sure that she would never see her family again. Several went to great length to change their plans and arrange sea travel, which meant that practically all the time of the leave would be used up. Some family tensions were so intensified that homes became fear-filled and distraught, and husband and wife relationships were at the breaking point. We became aware, as never before, of the terrific need for the perspective of what it means to walk "home" with Jesus, for this prospect is the perfect antidote for fear and the vital injection of faith.

Let's stop and take a look at *time* and Jesus' relationship to it. As descriptive a name for him as we can have is the "Eternal Now." He always has been and always will be. With him there is no past or present or future. That is why Scripture says: "Jesus Christ is the same yesterday and to-day and for ever" (Hebrews 13:8). This is what is included in the name he uses for himself: "I Am." It is why the Apostle Paul can say: "If we live, we live to the Lord, and if we die, we die to the Lord; so then, whether we live or whether we die, we are the Lord's" (Rom. 14:8). One of the wonderful things about this kind of faith is that it gives greater meaning to life here and now, too, for this is a part of eternity, not something separate from it.

In fact, this life takes on tremendous significance in that it is here that we make the conscious choice of accepting Christ and his gift of salvation or rejecting it. When we accept it and get a small glimpse of the love of God that it witnesses to, the full revelation of him that we will know in our eternal home becomes a prospect devoutly to be desired. Daily to sense that you are already here and now walking in eternity gives a significance to passing time that should make us good stewards.

In burying their dead, the Hebrews wrapped the bodies in garments and bound their heads with towels. These they called the "traveling clothes." When a Christian has accepted the spotless robe of the righteousness of Jesus Christ as his very own, such a person is truly equipped with the proper traveling clothes—yes, for the "valley of the shadow of death," and so he needs fear no evil.

Something happens to your attitude about growing old when you get this perspective. It is the time closer to "going home." How we look forward with such anticipation for our earthly home! What great things our heavenly Father has in store for us when we come "home"! No wonder Browning could write:

> Grow old along with me;
> The best is yet to be;
> The last of life for which the first was made.
> Our times are in His hands who said:
> "A whole I planned; youth shows but half.
> Trust God, see all, nor be afraid."
>
> "Rabbi Ben Ezra"
> BY ROBERT BROWNING

What is our heavenly home like? Scripture gives us a few glimpses but gathers it all up in the words: "What no eye has seen, nor ear heard, nor the heart of man conceived, what God has prepared for those who love him" (1 Cor. 2:9). There are no human words to describe the home God is readying for us!

The other night I was looking through some *National Geographic* magazines, and reveling in the wonders of creation. Here in Malaysia were flowers as big as bathtubs and of the most exotic forms. And so it was from one country to another: scenes of ineffable beauty that hardly seemed real. We have been privileged to travel a great deal, yet how little of the world we have actually seen. How little of the wonders of God's beautiful creation we really know! Then the thought came: this is why we need eternity. Apart from sin, we will be able to enjoy the wonder of God and all the things his mighty, loving hand has made.

Often, as a young girl, I used to think: "Oh, but I wish God had given me a lovely singing voice. How I would have used it to praise him!" Then I remembered what the late Dr. C. J. Sodergren said once at a Bible camp. He said: "Put a cross over every buried hope which has not been fulfilled in this life, and in Christ and according to God's promises, you will know there will be a resurrection in eternity." All of our unfulfilled desires for those things which make for real happiness, all the longings of our hearts will find their resurrection! What a prospect!

Not always is it given to those who are left behind to see a glimpse of the glory ahead in the lives of loved ones. Sometimes we grovel in the dark through days and weeks of the agony of the soul releasing itself from the shell of the body as we stand helplessly by. But there are times, when, as it were, the veil of heaven is drawn apart for a moment and we glimpse the glory beyond. Such was our experience at our mother's bedside; and in a less dramatic way, at Dad's homegoing too.

Dad had been sick only a week, and had gone to the hospital for an examination. It was the last day in the church year that Saturday evening when he called for the pastor to bring him holy Communion. He had been praying: "Come, Lord Jesus." As we gathered about his bedside in the hospital, to participate with him in this Sacrament of the Altar, the room became a place of light and hope and joy. The peace that was evident in him as he lay back on the pillow I can never forget. The next morning he had his "advent" as the first day of the church year dawned. We could but rejoice.

A year and a half later, our mother was in the hospital under an oxygen tent. Her heart had grown so big with trying to expend itself for others that no longer was there any elasticity in the muscles. It was worn out. There were eight of her ten children living, and we were all gathered at her bedside, having come from near and far. She motioned to the nurse to remove the apparatus. There we saw her white hair crowning that strong face with the wrinkles that the quick sense of humor had left on her face; there were those blue, blue eyes that were reminiscent of the lakes and oceans she loved so well; and there was her voice (could it possibly be) clear and strong and unwavering, singing, as she looked at each one of us in turn: "God be with you till we meet again." The window of heaven opened to fill the room with a golden glow, and we could but wish our be-loved, fun-loving, generous, big-hearted mother, journeying mercies, and the prospect of a grand reunion when there would be no more partings.

With the words: "Just as I am, without one plea, But that thy blood was shed for me" she had put her hand in the hand of Christ, and bidding us to do the same, looked for-ward to the time when we would all be together again.

A missionary tells the story of a former Muslim who had become a Christian. The friends of this convert asked him: "How come? Why did you choose to follow Christ rather than the Prophet Mohammed?" The man answered: "Well, it is like this. You are walking down the road and come to a fork in it. There are two roads leading in different ways.

At the end of one road is a dead man; at the end of the other is a living one. Aren't you foolish to choose the road that leads to the dead man?"

Friend, do you know this Christ who is for this life and for eternity; who is the *Eternal Now?* Do you know the security and peace that he will give to any soul who comes to him? Why don't you right now say: "Jesus, I take your gift; I accept you. I want to have all eternity with you!" There will be rejoicing in heaven. I like the words of the late Dag Hammarskjold as recorded in the book *Markings:* "Do not seek death; death will find you. But seek the road which makes death a fulfillment."

Travel Guides

1. Write down your thoughts about death. How do they differ from the views of those who have no hope?

2. Gather from Scripture all the promises of immortality.

3. Gather those passages that describe our heavenly home.

4. What often is pagan about so-called Christian funerals?

5. What in Christ's life is the "Amen" to our hope of everlasting life?

Prayer

Great Trailblazer, take my hand and lead me all the way. Make eternity alive here and now in my life. May I be "Looking upward, travel homeward to you, unafraid." Amen.

CHAPTER FOURTEEN

To the Ends of the Earth

"But thanks be to God, who continually leads us about, captives in Christ's triumphal procession, and everywhere uses us to reveal and spread abroad the fragrance of the knowledge of himself! We are indeed the incense offered by Christ to God, both for those who are on their way to salvation, and for those who are on the way to perdition: to the latter it is a deadly fume that kills, to the former a vital fragrance that brings life" (2 Cor. 2:14-16 NEB).

Here is one of the most inclusive sections of Scripture, and one so incisive as to make us rethink our entire "missionary" approach. So often, we who haven't experienced the world mission perspective sit at home and think in terms of "foreign" (I have come to hate the word) missions as something particularly holy; we sanctimoniously send our money so that our missionaries can bring the Gospel to the "poor heathen," and we act like venomous pagans to people of the same color who want to become our next-door neighbors. What we give off is a stench rather than a fragrance, and its bad odor reaches around the world! What does it mean to walk where Jesus walks—to the ends of the earth?

There is involved a quality of life that doesn't need to be jet-propelled—it breathes! It breathes into the place where you live, into your neighborhood, your office, the schoolroom, and to the farthermost corner of the world. It breathes through your thinking, your speech, your actions, your stewardship, your concern. It is the real you, Christ-captive! It is God's love channeling through you wherever you are. It is the hope of the world.

How often people try to cover up a bad odor with a dousing of perfume! You know how ineffective this is. But perfume on a clean body gives off its lovely fragrance and makes breathing sweet. So, often, in our spiritual lives, we have tried to cover the inner rottenness of self and pride and ambition with a spiritual sanctity that may fool a few people for a while, but which God sees through and loathes. "Clean the inside of the cup," were the words that Jesus threw at the Pharisees. "You are whited sepulchres," he said to them.

What is this quality that makes the difference? It is for Christ to so take over the whole of us that his love breathes out of everyone we meet. It is as Gertrude Behenna so effectively says in her record "God isn't dead!"—there should be a light in each of us that would be discernible as we walked down the street, as we entered a room, as we stopped to talk, that would make people pause to say: "Wow!" In our sophisticated manner we have done everything to obliterate this "difference"; in the selfish protection of our own interests, we have often buried the Flower whose fragrance could make the real difference in the lives of people!

Think about those with whom you have come into contact today, or this last week. Include everyone, from those whom you have invited as guests, to the man who services you in one way or another. Maybe it is the fellow at the cash register in the supermarket or the attendant at the gasoline station. Maybe it is the child that you casually bumped into on the street. How did you look at them? As someone who could be a convenience or an inconvenience to you, depending on how well they served you? As someone who interrupted your plans and so "put you out"? Has there been any awareness of each one's being a soul that Jesus Christ, your Savior, died to redeem?

I have seen women in a prayer group snarl at a servant in a most impatient and unfragrant way because of some irritation by noise in the performing of household duties on the part of their servant. It is almost as if there are two levels of life, or three: those we give ourselves to with all the warmth of our personality; those to whom we are indifferent; and those who please us if they serve us, but irritate us if they don't, according to the way that we think it ought to be done.

How interested are you in what the other fellow has to say to you, in what concerns him? I confess that there have been times when I could hardly wait to jump into the conversation with my "two bits' worth" so that I was not even hearing anyone else.

How can we counteract this "stinky self" that fills the world with strife and tension and bigotry and selfishness and everything else that makes for war?

We can't—but the grace of Jesus Christ can. It means a daily, down-on-the-knees saying: "Lord, crucify the self in me that gets in your way. Give me your spirit that makes me interested in everyone. Show me, Lord, how to let your fragrance breathe out through me." Then he will give you some practical helps. As you turn to search the Bible for directives, he will say: "Do nothing from selfishness or conceit, but in humility count others better than yourselves. Let each of you look not only to your own interests, but also to the interests of others" (Phil. 2:3-5). Or, "I appeal to you . . . to present your bodies as a living sacrifice, holy and acceptable to God." "Let love be genuine . . . outdo one another in showing honor . . . do not be overcome by evil, but overcome evil with good" (Romans 12). Has this been our perspective in our mission program as we have sought to share our Christ with the world?

Dr. John Seamands, former missionary to India, tells the story of a Christian worker in one of the Muslim states of Africa. The missionary was making a long trip by car in the company of a Muslim servant. He tried, as they rode along, to explain to the servant the main truths of the Christian faith, but seemed to make very little impact on him. The car developed mechanical trouble, and they had to pull off the highway for repairs. They tried to flag down a passing truck, wherein were two Africans, to ask for help, but the driver only grinned and moved along with an "it serves you right" attitude to this western intruder. After some time and a great deal of trouble the missionary was able to get his car moving again and they sped on their way.

But before long they came to the lorry stuck in the mud off the highway. "Ah," chortled the Muslim servant gleefully, "now we can pay these fellows back in kind. They passed us up; and now we'll pass them up." "Oh, no," said the missionary, "we must stop and help these men."

After they had given aid and were on their way, the boy turned to the missionary and said, "Sir, now I begin to understand something of the difference this Christ makes." He had breathed in the fragrance of Christ on an African road.

What a contrast this is to the experience an African friend of ours related one night! The bitterness it had left in the soul of the teller haunted us. As a young prospective seminary student he had been invited to a city some distance from his school, where he was to be the house guest of a missionary. When he went to the bathroom he found it locked. Instead he was directed to use the outside facilities! Only the redemptive grace of Christ will suffice to wipe out the pussy rancor that now filled his heart. He carried away a stench from that home.

A stripe of another sort is the story of "Praying Hyde" of India. Myra Scovel in her book *Richer by India* tells the fascinating account of this remarkable and different man. He gathered around himself a group of promising men to pledge themselves to voluntary poverty in order to serve the people about them better. He gave everything he owned to the poor, and when he gave his overcoat and bedding away, he would give away the blanket on the next bed, never thinking that the lady of the house might object. When he went to visit the sick and found the children dirty, he would get a basin and towel and wash the children's feet. (A memory stirs of another One . . . .) He had a delightful sense of humor. One day a rather worldly lady thought that she would have fun at his expense, so she asked him if he thought a lady who danced would go to heaven. Quickly he replied, "I don't see how a lady could go to heaven and not dance!"

Some missionaries became so exasperated at his failure to keep records and attend committee meetings that they wrote to the New York Board and asked them to recall him. They concluded their sorry list of grievances with: "All he ever does is pray." The cable which the mission board sent back was short and to the point: "Let him pray." As Mrs. Scovel suggests, one wonders how he would have passed the psychological and other tests that are used to help boards select qualified personnel today! Yet this one man so breathed the fragrance of his Lord and Master Jesus Christ that succeeding generations in India today call him blessed. And you should read about how God answered his prayers!

Any unusual quality of the fragrance of Christ is identification with those you seek to help. This is a simple projection of our creedal doctrine of incarnation. Christ has no preferred people. There are no V.I.P.'s in the kingdom of heaven. He belongs to everyone alike, and if we have in us the mind that is in Christ Jesus, we must see in every human being a brother, one whom Christ died to redeem. As the Epistle of John reads: "If any one says, 'I love God,' and hates his brother, he is a liar; for he who does not love his brother whom he has seen, cannot love God whom he has not seen. And this commandment we have from him, that he who loves God should love his brother also" (1 John 4:20, 21).

I am grateful to a friend for the idea of "shooting" prayers across to people. You have no idea what an adventure this can be until you have tried it. It works on a bus, in an airport, in a living room, or wherever. You can "shoot" prayers around the world. Do you know what they do? They blast open the hard ground that prevents the seed of God's Word from taking root. Prayers fuelled with the love of God can make amazing time, and do greater things than ever we can ask or think.

To pray intelligently we must be informed. To be a part of God's answer to the fields of the world, we ought to know what the situations are like. How much do you bestir yourself to become an aware Christian? Has your concept of missions undergone any maturing and growth since you first became interested? Make your knowledge personal; see these people for whom you pray as members of your own family. Get maps and become aware of the geography of the world! It is an insult to a Tanzanian for you to ask him to tell you about Africa. Africa is a continent of ever so many differing nations. But he can tell you about his own, Tanzania. Be informed.

Are you more interested in the foods they eat, and the animals that roam their wastes, than in the people struggling to get to their feet to declare their own personhood and identity? What is it that you want your missionaries on furlough to share? Are you impatient and quick to judge and repudiate, because these emerging immature countries make mistakes? Do you want to be protected from the unpleasant facts of starvation and malnutrition and disease because they make you uncomfortable? How different the fragrance of Christ in a person who would make these words his own:

> While there is a soul in prison, I am not free.
> While there is a child hungry, I am not fed.
> While there is a naked one shivering, I am not clothed.
> While there is a soul without hope, there is no peace.

As I look about the oil camp which was my home for several years, I realize that I sometimes became dreadfully impatient with women who were forever finding fault with things and doing nothing but entertaining themselves. But thank God, there were others who really expended their lives seeking to lift the standards of living, sharing with people in the villages. They would attend classes in Arabic to acquire some little knowledge of the language in order to communicate better. Then they became a part of that band of splendid volunteers who canvassed the hospital wards with sewing material for the Arab women, teaching them to sew *thobes* for their children, and blankets for their babies. Another group would go into the children's ward and play with the convalescing to help make the long hours shorter. Still another contingent went weekly to a model home to teach young wives and mothers wholesome nutrition and sanitation. Others accompanied the paid employee (who was proficient in Arabic) as they systematically covered a series of villages with films on hygiene, sanitation, and the prevention and treatment of prevalent diseases. Because as yet there was no electricity, a generator had to be brought along in order to make these lessons visual.

I feel compelled to give this witness: With all that has been written and said about *The Ugly American,* we have experienced in the attitude and concern of this company something so positively different that it thrilled me. (We were not in the employ of this group. We were independently serving the Protestant Fellowship and employed by them.) The Home Ownership Plan, the Agricultural Program, the impetus to education, and a remarkable medical program—all were other facets of concern to help an emerging people.

It is true that these are all secular programs, but is compassion secular? From where did it spring? I thrill to the insight of the famous Teilhardt de Chardin that the *élan vital* of all uplift and progress is the living Christ. Too often the shame is that Christian people will not give themselves to these efforts and therefore miss an opportunity to let their lives shine. Surely the ground of resistance to the love of Christ is broken by loving concern for the physical needs as well as the need of the soul. This is where the fragrance of love comes in. I have experienced it even across language barriers in a most powerful way. There is nothing others can discern as fast as whether or not you really care for them.

I would not minimize the witness of the many who served as church school teachers, in the department of church music, on the council, and on countless committees. God rewards with joy such service. But he expects us also to be the fragrance that permeates the community around us.

A friend told about her experience with a young man from Pakistan who worked in the same office as she did. This woman just had experienced a recommitment to Christ and was asking for grace to live him in every relationship. Her kindness to this co-worker, her enlivened concern about his family and his problems brought about a fine rapport. Reared in the Muslim faith, he had been watching her. Then one day he said: "You really believe your Jesus will help you, don't you?" He was fully aware of some of the trials through which she was passing. When she responded, "He has never failed me," the young man said, "I would like to read about him." She then turned to us for an Arabic New Testament (her friend was well versed in this language, for the Koran was written in it) and gave this to him. Consequently it became his greatest treasure and he is diligently reading it. We claim the promise of the Lord that his Word will not return void.

The fragrance of Christ? We saw it in the love of a friend who three times a week took a little polio victim to the swimming pool. She had the joy of seeing him make the first movements with his spindly legs, of seeing him gain enough strength to swim across the pool. Now through the help of friends she has been able to get him a stand-still bicycle so that in the months when the pool is closed he can continue his exercises. The joy the lad knows at being able to move those wheels is indescribable.

There is the good news of God's help in the classroom. A teen-ager explained to a teacher what tough going she had in her tests. She would study and be able to recite in class but she would "freeze" in a test. Quietly the teacher said to her: "Have you ever tried to pray about it? If you study well, then when you come to the test, you just take time to ask God to keep you calm and to share the knowledge you know." Two weeks later the girl with face aglow returned to her teacher friend. "My marks are better," she said, "God helped!" The joy she radiated was unmistakable, the fragrance of the enabling presence of God.

A year or two ago we were privileged to travel around the world, and to stop and enjoy Christian fellowship in many places. Girdling the globe with Christ is about as thrilling an experience as one can have. Will we ever forget that Church School Teachers' retreat in the little town in the

Bofu district in Japan? We sat on mats and ate our delicious "meal in one" rice concoction with our chopsticks. That was fun! But what an awkward hippopotamus I am on the floor! Then there was the sharing of our faith in Christ and the witness of his enabling, even under the most difficult circumstances, where people are so engrossed in material development that there hardly seems time for the things of the spirit. (Does that ring a bell about another country you know?) We sang together "How great thou art," and had a foretaste of a united choir singing praises to the Lamb.

Again, what a joy was a little personal retreat we had with a few missionaries, in a home where the American mother was attending the Japanese school with her very young daughters to learn the language more readily so that she could better serve. The fragrance of Christ was in that home.

In Taipei we were overwhelmed with Christian hospitality. We were the guests of our Chinese "son" who had lived with us for almost a year in the United States, as well as of a bank director who had been in and out of our church and home. Eleven different people in that city had shared our hospitality in the United States and now outdid themselves to return the kindness. This is something that we never dreamed would happen!

Again to feel the vibrant work with youth in the great center right across from one of the large universities, to share our witness with 100 of them on a Saturday night, to see the love and devotion they gave the Americans who were working in their midst—the fragrance of Christ!

Three stories from this experience I like to call the stories of the "Ones." Each is the story of one dedicated woman moving out to do what she could with what she had in her hand. The first woman is the wife of the head of a seminary. Seeing need all about her, she reached out to start to alleviate it. She found there were young girls who had no place to have their babies, and so she established a program of "Rooms for Mary." In a storehouse which we visited they were packing babies' layettes, to accompany the kindness of a place for a child to be born. She found there were young boys getting into trouble on the streets, and so, besides planning a camping program for them, she started them out in gainful occupation by having them stencil paper napkins. She discovered there were many unwanted old people aimlessly wandering on the streets, and through answered prayer she has been able to provide some shelter and joy for them. When we pressed her to find out how many had really come under her loving care, she admitted that she perhaps "put to bed" about 1,500 each night. The fragrance of Christ dominated every activity in the musty old warehouse where old clothing was being sorted and packed.

I wish I could adequately share with you the picture of another lady in Taipei. She had two children of her own to take care of besides her husband, but one day, looking out into the street, she saw a couple of orphaned children with no place to go. She took them in, and each day she found more. Pretty soon she had to ask her husband and children to move next door. Today she heads this tremendous orphanage which often takes children no other institution will accept because of physical disability or mental retardation. Some three hundred children are under the roof which the wives of the military personnel of the United States have provided. They also do voluntary work in this institution to keep this great work of love going. To see the children gather around this little woman with the big heart is to breathe in the presence of Jesus Christ. Laughter and happiness abounded in that place.

The third woman we did not get to meet, but her story is a saga of the ingenuity God gives people to keep his work going. When the Japanese took over during the war, the military tried to weed out all Christian work, because they associated it with their enemy. A native Formosan wasn't to be daunted. When the missionaries had to leave, she was left with a supply of tracts and single books of the Bible. The enemy forces tried every way they could to track her down as she went into the mountains from village to village sharing her literature. Always there were those who were clever enough to hide her.

She wasn't lacking in ingenuity herself. One day she slipped on a certain train and had been followed by spies. They alerted soldiers at the first stop to be on the lookout for her. But word had come to the train's engineer about what was about to happen, so he stopped at a tiny little path and left this soldier of Jesus Christ out. When the Japanese searched the train at the appointed stop, they couldn't understand what had happened to her.

When the war was over and the missionaries began to come back, they found village after village ripe for a church with people asking to be baptized. One intrepid soul had walked through those mountain fastnesses with the fragrance of Jesus Christ.

Who can adequately describe Christ's love as it breathes out through the streets of Hong Kong? Surplus American flour being made into noodles for nutritional food, homeless refugee girls established in a home, gainfully employed knitting beautiful sweaters (six of these girls were blind, and one had but one arm, but could they knit!); a home for blind children as inviting and beautiful as I have seen anywhere; help with housing and food and clothes and the wherewithal to get started in a gainful occupation; and the good news of the love of Christ spread through the schools, through the churches, through the seminary and the Bible school with the all-pervading air of the perfume of loving compassion. Christ walks those streets in human flesh, and though a word of direct witness may possibly not be spoken, the fragrance of his presence is unmistakable.

Will we ever forget the warmth of love with which we were surrounded, and that band of missionaries who saw us off to Indonesia? We were unwillingly headed for Djakarta, although we wanted only to go to Sumatra, and this round-about route was the only one left open. Our grandson was to be baptized that Sunday. Medan in Sumatra is over a thousand miles from Djakarta. We went on faith, asking God to open the way, carrying along a thermos jug with ice containing polio vaccine and other inoculations that we hoped would protect our little lad from disease. The week before, the British Embassy had been burned, and we sensed that we were not too welcome in the capital city. But the prayers of the Hong Kong friends had gone before, and late on Saturday night we arrived in Medan. By this time the folks had given up all hope of our coming. (The cable we sent from Hong Kong long days before arrived three days after we ourselves had arrived in Siantar.) Again kind friends opened the way and we drove into Siantar about 11 P.M. that Saturday evening.

We had been in Sumatra in Indonesia two years before on a like visit to our daughter, so we knew something of its tropical beauty, and had then experienced warm love and acceptance in Christian fellowship. It is something to travel through that island of Sumatra and see cross-topped steeples lift their spires in practically every village. The hospital, the school for the blind, the trade school, the leprosarium, plus the many regular schools conducted by the indigenous church, and the seminary of Nommensen all witness to the transforming power of the love of Christ through a century.

I'll never forget climbing up the ladder to the low entrance of one of the colorfully decorated sway-back homes on stilts, and there through an interpreter sharing in prayer and singing the glorious hymn: "Praise to the Lord, the Almighty, the King of creation." The fragrance of Christ was there in the little mother who presided over that domicile with the sounds of chickens and pigs underneath coming through the worn boards of the floor. She took our hands warmly, and as her eyes shone, tried to express what it means to experience this fellowship in Christ. Amidst the Malaysian-Indonesian conflict, the tumult within and without the church, thank God for the reality of the fragrance of the presence of Jesus Christ in these nations around the world. It is indeed to those who "are on the way to perdition a deadly fume that kills, but to those who are on their way to salvation it is a vital fragrance that brings life."

Can I ever erase from my mind the sight of our loved ones standing at the airport to wave us goodbye, with their little baby in their arms? There were so many miles and such international obstacles to separate us! What a gift is prayer, and how it draws us together at the throne of the

Lamb! Through the aching heart came the voice of the One
I love: "Lo, I am with you always, even unto the end of the
world" (Matt. 28:20 KJV).

In Bangkok we were overwhelmed with the fabulous
temples reared to the Emerald Gods, to the God of the
Dawn, and countless others. The obese, grotesque figures
representing these "deities" made one want to cry out with
the Apostle Paul on Mars Hill in Athens: "God that made
the world and all things therein, seeing that he is Lord of
heaven and earth, dwelleth not in temples made with hands;
neither is worshipped with men's hands, as though he
needed any thing . . . . in him we live, and move, and have
our being" (Acts 17:24, 28 KJV). How can we as Christians
be so meager in our response to the God we know in Jesus
Christ? How thankful I was for the medical work and the
work among lepers besides the evangelical work in this fascinating country that were breathing out the spirit of
Christ! How I wished that it might be multiplied many
times over!

Then we were in India—the place that had so reached out
to me in college. I had loved the beauty of the poetry of Ta-
gore and the spiritual sensitivity of the gifted people. Now
I was here. The story of Dr. Ida Scudder had been a real
inspiration to this emerging young woman during the im-
pressionable years at college. Well, Vellore was no disap-
pointment. The fragrance of Christ is there! Many of our
nurses in Dhahran had been trained there, so I knew something of the caliber and spirit of the training they received.
The beloved friend, Dr. Ruth Myers, who was our hostess,
may have had a crippled leg, but this didn't deter her from
setting such a pace for us as was hard to follow. This is the

way she gave her whole life—in the laboratory, where God had gifted her with a brilliant mind to search out the secrets of healing through research; in the classroom, where each student was special; in her home where she shared hospitality so generously.

We followed the mobile bus one morning to see how the work of the hospital was being carried right into the country. Brother James, with his arrested case of leprosy (part of one foot was taken by the disease before he was able to get medication), was there with his violin and shared the Gospel message by the roadside with those who were waiting for treatment. He could tell firsthand what the coming of Jesus Christ has meant in his life. On every hand there was evidence of the transforming power of our wonderful Savior. The air was fragrant and redolent with his presence.

It seemed like a miracle to have one name after the other that had been a part of my prayers through the years come alive and be a place and people. The seminary at Madras, the hospital and work at Bhimavaram, the hospital and many-faceted work at Rajahmundry, the advanced work at Guntur, the beautiful work with the blind at Rentachintala, and that isolated, lonely outpost on the road to Hyderabad where a warm-hearted nurse was dedicating her life to the health and welfare of the surrounding community. What an essence we carried with us from her presence!

I wish everyone could meet Hilda, the teacher of the deaf at Rajahmundry. She is over 70 years old. You have never seen such sprightliness in your life as she would hold up the charts and put the fingers of her pupils to feeling her throat, as she put words together, thus unlocking the shut door of their tongues. Joy abounded in that classroom, where the teaching was punctuated with a tweak of the nose, or a gentle pull of the ear. The nimble feet of the septuagenarian tapped out the rhythm of what she was trying to teach so that, though they could not hear it, they could still feel the vibrations. That was one of the most remarkable hours in a classroom that I have ever spent. The air had in it the scent of eternity. Life was in it, and *love*.

We saw the presence of the Christ, too, in the faces of the Bible school girls with whom we worshipped that Sabbath morning in Guntur. I wish I could show you the slide of them coming out of the church. It's radiant! By the way, how do you look when you have been worshipping our Lord?

Though we could not understand the language, we were aware of the text the humble man of God used when he broke the Bread of Life for these people that Sabbath morning. The time passed quickly as we used it to remember each worshipper in prayer. We carried away with us the symbol of the pastor, garbed in his ecclesiastical robes, and barefooted. Yes, the ground on which he had been standing was holy!

Breathe deeply, friend, as you trace the footprints of Christ around the world. The atmosphere is filled with the crushed flower of his Calvary giving, and repeated in human beings who are dedicated to following him. Are you a part of this great procession?

Travel Guides

1. Plan a study of the various mission opportunities your church supports.

2. Plan a pattern of prayer for these.

3. Face yourself with the question: Is the essence of my life the love of Christ for everybody?

4. Do you permit his love to flow through you?

5. What opportunities for this expression might there be close at hand that you have not availed yourself of?

Prayer

Everywhere around the world where you have been, Lord, there is evidence of your fragrance. Thank you for those who channel it to the lives of the sick and maimed and wounded and forgotten. Uphold them with the joy of your presence. Use me, Lord, to be a part of this kind of a climate where I am. Amen.

CHAPTER FIFTEEN

Epilogue

" . . . forgetting what lies behind, and straining forward to what lies ahead, I press on toward the goal for the prize of the upward call of God in Jesus Christ" (Phil. 3:13, 14).

How often I remember hearing my beloved mother say: "If I only had my life to live over again!" This we are not given to do, but we are given the opportunity of *today,* of beginning where we are, and with the impowering of the Holy Spirit catching step with our Lord. As I have been going over these pages, there is a little couplet that haunts me:

> Only one life; 'twill soon be past;
> Only what's done for Christ will last.

Where are you going? Whom are you following? What is your goal?

"And this is my prayer, that your love may grow ever richer and richer in knowledge and insight of every kind, and may thus bring you the gift of true discrimination. Then on the Day of Christ you will be flawless and without blame, reaping the full harvest of righteousness that comes

through Jesus Christ, to the glory and praise of God" (Phil.
1:9-11 NEB).

> Set us afire, Lord,
> Stir us, we pray.
> While the world perishes,
> We go our way,
> Purposeless, passionless,
> Day after day.
> Set us afire, Lord,
> Stir us, we pray.
>
> ANON.

Date Due

AUG 30 '89			